MEGHARIEF
POETRY ANTHOLOGY

About the Author

Dokali (Duke) Megharief, BBA, MBA, and PhD, is
a retired businessperson with extensive experience
in various industries, including oil and gas, real
estate development, the automobile industry,
general trading, asset management, and fintech. Over
his fifty-year career, he has distinguished himself as a
leader in these fields through his diverse business
experience. He is the author of several books, including
The Intellect Groups, The Prophecies Kid, The Santa
of Roses, The Legacy and Reflections of Table 77, and
three books on Leadership.

Megharief Poems Anthology

Introduction

Welcome to the enchanting world of *A Poetry Anthology*, a mesmerizing collection by Dokali Megharief. This anthology stands as a testament to innovative poetic creation, where each verse intricately weaves the fabric of a story, sometimes grounded in reality, sometimes soaring through the realms of fiction. These poems transcend the ordinary, inviting readers to immerse themselves fully in the vivid imaginations and scenarios crafted by the author.

This anthology explores an expansive array of themes through a diverse range of captivating stories, from the intimate details of everyday life on Earth to the boundless mysteries of galaxies far beyond. Every poem is a portal, guiding readers on a journey of exploration, reflection, and wonder. The unique method employed in these creations enables readers not only to understand but also to connect deeply with the underlying narratives, fostering the art of storytelling through poetry.

Embark on this literary adventure and let your imagination soar as you delve into the tales and verses that form the heart of *A Poetry Anthology*. Whether you seek to discover new worlds or find deeper meaning in familiar ones, this collection promises to inspire, enlighten, and captivate.

Let us delve into the background of this Poetry Anthology and get a glimpse of its related stories

PART ONE

The Voice of the Desert

The Voice of the Desert

Yousef, known as "The Voice of the Desert," was a unique child born in the desert who displayed extraordinary abilities from a very young age. He could communicate with the elements, predict nature's behaviors, and guide his people through the desert's harsh conditions.

His wisdom and influence extended far beyond the desert, contributing to the development of prosperous communities and promoting peace among the tribes. However, Yousef faced opposition from a power-hungry group called the Black Suits Council, who sought to exploit his abilities. Despite these challenges, Yousef stood firm, protecting the balance of the desert and the well-being of its inhabitants. His story is one of harmony, respect for nature, and the enduring legacy of a boy whose wisdom and guidance became legendary.

The story of Yousef is a rich and immersive narrative that explores profound themes of introspection, virtue, and resilience. It is a journey that delves deep into the human spirit, illuminating the path to a life of compassion, purpose, and integrity.

The prologue introduces us to a world where ancient wisdom and modern aspirations intersect. The elders, with their beards like snow, recognize Yousef as a vessel for secrets from time and space. They see in him a beacon of hope, someone destined to teach love, compassion, and wisdom to the people of his land.

The marketplace serves as a hub of fervent debate and trade. Scholars and merchants alike acknowledge Yousef's unique position as both sage and bridge between worlds. His words are treasured, seen as prophetic and laden with the weight of fate. Yousef stands as the prophecy's child, a wanderer who is both tamed and beguiled by his journey.

Yousef finds himself immersed in a faraway land, where he is woven into the very souls of its people. He becomes a messenger of hope, walking the streets with a clear purpose, dispelling fear and spreading wisdom. His journey is marked by moments of profound reflection, particularly under the twilight sky, where he questions his identity and purpose

Who am I?

Born in the desert's arid embrace,
A child of sun and sand, I trace

The ancient whispers carried on the wind,
A language known to me since I descend.

At three months old, my lips formed words,
Fluent syllables, celestial chords,
A gift bestowed, divine and rare,
To speak the truth beyond compare.

I gazed upon the shifting dunes,
Saw futures dance like silver moons,
Predictions etched upon my soul
A seer's vision, my purpose whole.

Through scorching days and moonlit nights,
I wandered far, my heart alight,
Crossing borders, bridging seas,
Spreading love like a fragrant breeze.

Visions came to me in dreams,
A tapestry of fate's grand schemes,
Threads of destiny woven tight,
Guiding me toward the cosmic light.

Yet now I stand on foreign shores,
My footsteps echoing ancient lore,
And ask myself, with searching eyes,
"Who am I beneath these boundless skies?"

Am I a vessel for the stars' decree,
Or merely dust upon life's tapestry?
A wanderer lost or a beacon bright,
A seeker of truth in endless flight.

The prophecy within me grows,
A mystery only time may disclose,
But one thing remains, unwavering and true:
I am the desert's child, and I am you.

Wandering through realms of shifting sand,
I sought the heart of this enigmatic land.
The sun, my compass, the moon, my domified
, I journeyed on, my purpose amplified.

In ancient bazaars, I shared my lore,
Whispering secrets from the days of yore.
Merchants and beggars, kings and thieves,
All listened, spellbound, beneath the eaves.

I spoke of love that transcends the veil,
Of kindness sown in every dusty trail.
My words, like raindrops on parched earth,
Nourished souls, igniting rebirth.

Through bustling souks and silent dunes,
I wove a tapestry of forgotten tunes.
The boy who spoke with stars' refrain,
A bridge between realms, both joy and pain.

Yet as the years unfurled their wings,
I questioned the purpose that fate brings.
Who am I, really, beneath this guise?
A vessel for truth or a mere disguise?

Visions still danced behind my eyes,
Prophecies etched in twilight skies.

Nations rose and crumbled in my wake,
Their destinies woven in threads I'd make.

And so I wandered, seeking solace and signs,
Across deserts vast and oceanic brines.
The boy who spoke the language of stars,
Yearning for answers beyond earthly bars.

Now, as the sun dips low on the horizon,
I stand at the edge of existence's prison.
The prophecy whispers, a haunting refrain:
"You are the weaver, the dreamer, the rain."

And so I ask once more, beneath this sky:
Who am I, really, as the ages fly?
A wanderer lost or a beacon of grace.
Perhaps both, entwined in cosmic embrace.

The sun dips low, a golden kiss,
And shadows lengthen, secrets hiss.
Before me lies a vast expanse,
A canvas painted by chance.

Mountains rise like ancient kings,
Their crowns adorned with snowflake wings.
Valleys cradle whispered streams,
Where dreams are woven into seams.

I step across the threshold's brink,
Where time and space begin to sync.
The desert's heat gives way to cool,
As if the earth itself were a pool.

Stars emerge, their stories told,
In constellations, myths unfold.
The boy who speaks their sacred tongue,
Guided by their light since he was young.

I walk through forests thick with pine,
Where echoes of forgotten rhyme
Reside within each rustling leaf,
A symphony of life and grief.

Creatures watch me with curious eyes,
Their wisdom ancient, their hearts unwise.
They sense the prophecy's weight on my skin
And wonder what lies beyond my kin.

The moon ascends, a silver sail,
Its glow illuminates the trail.
I follow whispers on the breeze,
To where the ocean meets the trees.

Salt and sand blend in embrace,
As waves recite their endless grace.
The boy who crossed continents and seas,
Now stands at the edge of mysteries.

I close my eyes, inhale the night,
And feel the pulse of cosmic light.
Who am I? I ask once more,
A wanderer lost or a celestial door.

Perhaps both, the stars reply,
A bridge between earth and sky.

The prophecy within you sings,
A tale of boundless, eternal wings.

And so I step into the unknown,
A traveler with a heart fullblown.
Beyond the next horizon, I stride,
A seeker of truth, forever untied.

Who am I, this wanderer of old,
A prophet's voice, a tale untold?
Grown from desert sands to city streets,
Where knowledge blooms and temptation meets.

In Uruk's bustling heart, I tread,
A messenger with words unsaid.
The prophecy burns within my chest,
Yet civilization scoffs, unimpressed.

They gather in squares, their eyes averted,
Their hearts encased, their minds diverted.
"Who is this dreamer?" they whisper low,
As if my truth were but a fleeting glow.

I stand on corners, my voice a plea, "Listen,
O people, come learn from me!"
But they pass me by, their faces cold,
Their souls imprisoned, their hearts untold.

The scholars mock, their brows raised high,
"Prophecy? Nonsense!" they scoff and sigh.
Their ink-stained scrolls, their rigid rules,
Blind them to truths beyond their schools.

I trace the ancient lines of fate,
The tablets etched with visions great.
Yet they dismiss me, this boy unclaimed,
Lost in the labyrinth of minds untamed.

The elders frown, their beards like snow,
"Your words disrupt our status quo.
" They cling to power, their hearts grown small,
While I seek answers beyond their wall.

The city pulses, its heartbeat loud,
Yet my purpose eludes me, like a shroud.
Am I a vessel for the stars' decree,
Or a fool who dreams of what could be?

The streets echo with laughter and strife,
As I wander, seeking meaning in life.
The prophecy's weight upon my brow,
I question existence—then wonder how.

Perhaps I am the bridge between realms,
A thread connecting forgotten helms.
Or maybe I'm a mirage, a fleeting spark,
Lost in the chasm between light and dark.

The moon whispers secrets to the night,
As I grapple with purpose, seek insight.
The boy who once spoke with celestial fire,
Now adrift in a sea of doubt and desire.

I watch the city sleep, its dreams aglow,
And wonder if I'll ever truly know.
Who am I, this wanderer of fate?
A seeker of truth or a cosmic weight?

In distant lands where whispers bloom,
I found my refuge, my sacred room.
The boy who once wandered, lost and free,
Now stood before a crowd, eyes filled with glee.

They gathered 'round, their faces aglow,
Hungry for truths only prophets know.
Their hearts, like open books, yearned to read,
The language of stars, the celestial creed.

I spoke of visions etched in sand,
Of prophecies woven by fate's own hand.
"Listen," I said, "to the wind's refrain,
For truth lies hidden in every grain."

The elders nodded, their beards like snow,
Their eyes reflecting the ancient glow.
"This boy," they murmured, "is touched by grace,
A vessel for secrets from time and space."

The children danced, their laughter bright,
As I wove tales of day and night.
"The moon," I told them, "Whispers dreams,
And rivers carry the universe's streams."

The prophecy within me blazed anew,
A beacon of hope, a skyward view.
I taught them love, compassion, and more,
As if the desert winds had whispered lore.

The marketplace buzzed with fervent debate,
As scholars pondered their rigid slate.

"This boy," they argued, "is both sage and fool,
A bridge between worlds, a cosmic tool."

The merchants traded their gold and spice,
Their eyes reflecting the starlit ice.
"His words," they whispered, "are worth their weight,
In futures spun from the loom of fate."

And so I stood, the prophecies' child,
A wanderer tamed, yet still beguiled.
"Who am I?" I wondered, "beneath this sky?
A vessel of truth or a passing sigh?"

The faraway land embraced me whole,
Its people weaving me into their soul.
I walked their streets, my purpose clear,
A messenger of hope, dispelling fear.

But as the sun dipped low, shadows grew long,
I pondered my path, my purpose strong.
"Who am I?" I asked the twilight sky.
The answer came, with love's serene sigh: "You're
Yousef, the Prophecy Child.

PART TWO
AMIR`S LIFELONG JOURNEY

AMIR's Lifelong Story

The Literary Tapestry

As the narrative unfolds, we are guided through Amir's introspective journey. He is depicted as a character whose life is anchored by timeless values—humility, compassion, and integrity. The story celebrates these virtues, highlighting their transformative power.

The Transformative Power of Values

Each chapter of Amir's life emphasizes the importance of staying true to oneself. His experiences remind us of the profound impact of genuine empathy and steadfast principles on the world. Amir's journey serves as a beacon, encouraging readers to reflect on their values and navigate life with compassion and purposefully.

A Mirror of Human Virtues

Amir's tale is more than a recounting of events; it is an odyssey that probes the essence of living with honor and grace. His unwavering commitment to his morals, despite adversity, offers a profound lesson in resilience. Through moments of joy and hardship, his story becomes a testament to the enduring power of the human spirit.

Interactions and Justice

In his interactions with friends, family, and strangers, Amir's actions are driven by a deep-seated sense of justice and a fervent desire to improve the world. His journey often leads him into uncharted territories, where he must navigate complex social landscapes using his values. These moments reveal the depth of his empathy and wisdom.

Facing Darkness with Courage

The narrative does not shy away from life's darker aspects. Instead, it embraces them, showing how Amir confronts and overcomes challenges with courage and compassion. His story reminds us that greatness is not measured by the absence of struggle but by the grace with which one faces it. Through his trials, Amir emerges as a hero and a symbol of hope.

Conclusion

Amir's journey is a source of strength and reflects the virtues we hold dear. His story ignites a spark within us, encouraging us to live with greater empathy, integrity, and purpose. As we embark on this literary voyage, we discover, as Amir does, that the accurate compass of life is found within the heart.

Chapter One: Reflections on the Azure Sea

In the serene embrace of the azure sea, Amir finds a moment of profound introspection. This chapter sets the stage for his journey, with the vast ocean serving as a metaphor for the possibilities and challenges that lie ahead. Amir reflects on the ebb and flow of his life, drawing parallels between the sea's infinite depths and the depths of his own aspirations.

The sea's tranquil surface belies the turbulent currents below, much like Amir's calm exterior masks his intense passion for change and progress. As he gazes upon the horizon, the boundary between sea and sky becomes a symbol of the limitless potential he sees in himself and the world.

This chapter is not just an opening to Amir's story; it is an invitation to the reader to dive into the depths of their own reflections, to find solace in the stillness, and to muster the courage to navigate the uncharted waters of their dreams.

Upon the azure sea, so vast and wide,
Amir stands alone, with the tide as his guide.
The water whispers secrets, old and new,
A symphony of waves, in every hue.

The horizon stretches, endless and far,
A canvas of dreams, beneath the morning star.
Each ripple tells a tale of times to come,
Of battles to be fought, and victories won.

Reflections on the sea, a mirror of the soul,
Revealing hidden depths, making Amir whole.
The salt in the air, the breeze on his face,
In this moment of peace, he finds his place
.

The sea's a mentor, its lessons are clear,
Teachings of resilience, year after year.
It's here that Amir learns to be so brave,
Dancing with the dolphins, riding each wave.

The ocean, it calls, with its siren's song,
To sail beyond the right, to sail beyond the wrong.
In the depths of desire, where passions ignite,
Amir finds his purpose, in the sea's great might.

So cast off the lines, set the sails high,
Chart a course for dreams, under the open sky.
For life is an ocean, vast and profound,
And in the heart of the sea, our truths are found

Chapter Two: The Voyage of Values

As Amir embarks on his life's voyage, the guiding principles that form his moral compass are illuminated in this chapter. "The Voyage of Values" explores the core beliefs that guide Amir through life's tumultuous waters. His unwavering commitment to integrity, empathy, and resilience serves as the sails that propel him forward. At the same time, his dedication to justice and fairness acts as the anchor, grounding him in times of adversity. Amir's values are not just ideals; they are the stars by which he navigates, ensuring that every decision and action aligns with his ethical framework. This chapter reflects on how values shape our identity and influence our journey. It is a testament to the idea that while skills and knowledge can chart the course to success, our values will define the legacy we leave behind.

In the voyage of life, where values are the mast,
Amir sails forth, with virtues that will last.
With integrity as his compass, true and tried,
He charts a course where honor cannot hide.

The winds of wisdom fill his sails so wide,
Guiding him through storms, being his guide.
Empathy's the rudder, steering his heart's fleet,
Through oceans of sorrow and alleys bittersweet.

Amir's values whisper through the gale,
A chorus of truths that will prevail.
Justice is his anchor, deep and strong,
In the harbor of right, where he belongs.

Humility's the star by which he steers,
A constellation of modesty that appears.
In the darkest night, it shines so bright,
A beacon of humility in the blackest night.

The voyage of values, a journey so grand,
A testament to where his morals stand.
For Amir knows, as he traverses the sea,
It's the values he holds that will set him free

Chapter Three: The Compass of Compassion

In "The Compass of Compassion," Amir's journey is steered by his profound capacity for empathy and understanding. This chapter explores compassion's pivotal role in shaping his interactions and decisions. Amir's empathy is not passive; it is a dynamic force that drives him to take meaningful action, whether in personal relationships or broader social initiatives. His compassion is depicted as a guiding force that navigates him through life's complexities, enabling him to connect with others on a profound, human level.

This quality endears him to those around him and garners respect across various spheres of his life. The narrative illustrates how Amir's compassionate approach leads to impactful outcomes, fostering a culture of kindness and generosity. Through Amir's story, the chapter underscores the transformative power of compassion, suggesting that it is an essential virtue for navigating the human experience with grace and purpose.

In the voyage of life, where values are the mast,
Amir sails forth, with virtues that will last.
With integrity as his compass, true and tried,
He charts a course where honor cannot hide.

The winds of wisdom fill his sails so wide,
Guiding him through storms, being his guide.
Empathy's the rudder, steering his heart's fleet,
Through oceans of sorrow and alleys bittersweet.

Amir's values whisper through the gale,
A chorus of truths that will prevail.
Justice is his anchor, deep and strong,
In the harbor of right, where he belongs.

Humility's the star by which he steers,
A constellation of modesty that appears.
In the darkest night, it shines so bright,
A beacon of humility in the blackest night.

The voyage of values, a journey so grand,
A testament to where his morals stand.
For Amir knows, as he traverses the sea,
It's the values he holds that will set him free

Chapter Four: The Anchors of Altruism

Chapter Four portrays Amir as a beacon of empathy, with compassion serving as his guiding principle. His innate ability to understand and share the feelings of others is not merely a passive trait but an active impetus for change.

Amir's empathy fuels his commitment to social causes and personal relationships, allowing him to navigate life's challenges with a profound connection to those around him. This deep empathy earns him admiration and respect, as he consistently acts with kindness and generosity.

The chapter highlights the significant impact of Amir's compassionate actions, which ripple out to create a culture of caring and benevolence.

Through Amir's example, the narrative celebrates compassion as a transformative force, essential for leading a life of grace and purpose and inspiring others to do the same.

In the realm where heartbeats echo loud,
Amir walks among the bustling crowd.
With a compass of compassion in his hand,
He navigates the byways of the land.

The needle points to kindness, ever true,
A guiding light in everything he'd do.
With every step, he'd leave a gentle trace,
Of empathy in this human race.

In the eyes of strangers, he'd find kin,
For every soul, a story deep within.
He'd listen to the silent cries of need,
And to the call of compassion, he'd heed.

Through the alleys of anguish and the streets of strife,
Amir's compass led him through each life.
A beacon for the lost, the hurt, the small,
His heart, a haven, open to all.

So let us learn from Amir's tender ways,
To live with compassion all our days.

For in the end, it's love that will endure,
A compass true, in hearts that are pure.

Chapter Five: The Tides of Time

In "The Tides of Time," Amir navigates the ever-changing currents of life, reflecting on the impermanence and constant flux of his experiences. This chapter explores how Amir's life is shaped by the passage of time, with each moment bringing new challenges and opportunities. As he matures, Amir learns to embrace change, understanding that time's tides can bring both loss and gain. He witnesses the evolution of his dreams and ambitions, adapting his goals to the lessons learned with each high and low tide. Time's relentless march tests Amir's resilience, yet he finds strength in the knowledge that every ebb has its flow. The chapter emphasizes the importance of perseverance and adaptability, suggesting that one should ride the tides of time with courage and foresight. Amir's story becomes a metaphor for the human condition, where time is both a formidable adversary and a valuable ally.

Upon the shores of life, where time does ebb and flow,
Amir stands watchful as the tides come and go.
The sands of moments past slip through his grasp,
Yet in his heart, the future's hand he'll clasp.

The tides of time, they rise, they fall, they turn,

With every cycle, a new lesson to learn.
Amir rides the waves, through years that swiftly fly,
Underneath the ever-changing sky.

The past's a ship that's sailed, its journey done,
The present's gift is here, not to be shunned.
The future's tide is coming, vast and wide,
Amir prepares to take it in his stride.

For time is like the sea, deep and immense,
Its tides can carry us past every fence.
Amir knows well, with every high and low,
The tides of time help us to grow.

So let us sail these tides with open eyes,
Embrace the change, as time soars and flies.
For in the tides of time, we find our way,
To new horizons, with each breaking day.

Chapter Six: The Winds of Wisdom

"Chapter Six: The Winds of Wisdom" captures Amir's intellectual journey as he harnesses the winds of knowledge to sail towards enlightenment. Wisdom, for Amir, is not merely acquired; it is a force that propels him forward, shaping his decisions and guiding his actions. This chapter illustrates Amir's pursuit of understanding, driven by an insatiable curiosity and a deep desire to grasp the world's complexities. His experiences become his compass, and the lessons learned are the gusts that fill his sails. Amir's wisdom is shared generously, impacting those around him and leaving a trail of insight in his wake.

The narrative emphasizes that wisdom is not static but a dynamic process of growth and discovery. Amir's story encourages embracing lifelong learning, suggesting that the winds of wisdom are always there, ready to be caught by those who are willing to set their minds adrift on the quest for knowledge.

In the library of life where silence reigns,
Amir seeks the wisdom that each book contains.
With every page he turns, the winds arise,
Whispering secrets of the old and wise.

Through scrolls of knowledge, his journey's spun,
A quest for truth that's never truly done.
The winds of wisdom, how they gust and swirl,
Around this seeker in the scholarly whirl.

He charts a course through history's vast domain,
Where ancient voices echo, not in vain.
In every tale and theorem, he finds clues,
To navigate life's vast and varied hues.

The gales of insight push him to explore,
Beyond the comfort of the familiar shore.
With wisdom's wind beneath his eager sails,
Amir discovers truths that never fails.

So let us catch these winds, so wild and free,
That blow from the mountains to the sea.
For in the winds of wisdom, we shall find,
The power to enlighten humankind.

Chapter Seven: The Currents of Connection

This chapter delves into the profound relationships that Amir forges throughout his life. These connections are not mere interactions but powerful currents influencing his journey, providing support and direction. Amir's ability to connect with others on a deep level is highlighted as one of his greatest strengths. He cultivates relationships with care, recognizing the mutual benefits of strong bonds.

This chapter portrays Amir as a confluence where various streams of life meet, each connection contributing to the river of his experiences.

His empathy and genuine interest in others' well-being create lasting ties, and his network becomes a source of strength and wisdom.

The narrative emphasizes the importance of human connections in navigating life's challenges and achieving success. Amir's story is a reminder that the currents of connection are vital to personal growth and fulfillment, shaping our paths in profound ways

In the river of life where currents flow,
Amir finds a connection, a warm, gentle glow.
With every handshake, every heartfelt smile,
He weaves a tapestry, mile after mile.

The currents of connection, strong and deep,
Carry him forward, through waters wide and steep.
Each soul he meets, a story to unfold,
In the book of life, their tales are told.

A bridge of understanding, he builds with care,
Spanning the gaps, through the air so rare.
With every bond, the current grows more clear,
Uniting hearts, drawing them so near.

In the flow of friendship, he finds his grace,
A confluence of minds, a sacred space.
The currents of connection do not wane,
Through joy and sorrow, love, and pain.

So let us sail these waters, hand in hand,
Creating ripples across the land.
For in the currents of connection, we find,
The unity of humankind.

Chapter Eight: The Storms of Struggle

"Chapter Eight: The Storms of Struggle" presents Amir's resilience in the face of life's inevitable adversities. The chapter uses the storm metaphor to depict the tumultuous periods that Amir encounters, emphasizing the internal and external conflicts he must weather.

These struggles range from personal doubts to professional setbacks, each storm testing Amir's resolve and pushing him to his limits. Despite the ferocity of these challenges, Amir's spirit remains unbroken. He learns to navigate through these storms, drawing on his deep reserves of strength and the support of his connections.

The narrative portrays struggle as an essential part of growth, a force that, while daunting, can lead to greater wisdom and fortitude. Amir's journey through the storms becomes a powerful lesson in perseverance, showing that it is not the absence of struggle but the

ability to persevere through it that defines true
strength.

In the heart of the tempest, Amir stands tall,
Against the howling winds, he will not fall.
The storms of struggle, fierce and wild,
Test the mettle of this gentle child.

With thunderous roars and lightning's flash,
The skies above with turmoil clash.
Yet Amir's spirit, like a sturdy mast,
Holds fast against the furious blast.

The gales of hardship try to break his will,
But in the storm's eye, he finds a thrill.
For every challenge, every strife,
Carves the strength into his life.

Through torrents of trials that life does brew,
Amir's resolve is steadfast, and his courage is true.
He rides the storms, no matter how rough,
For diamonds are made from stuff this tough.

So let us learn from Amir's rugged fight,
To stand our ground with all our might.
For in the storms of struggle, we too can find,
The power to persevere, the will to shine.

Chapter Nine: The Horizons of Hope

In Chapter Nine: The Horizons of Hope, Amir's narrative turns toward the future, focusing on the bright prospects that lie ahead.

This chapter portrays Amir's unwavering optimism, even in the face of daunting challenges. His hope is likened to the horizon, ever-present and promising, a reminder that beyond the darkest clouds, the sun still shines. Amir's hope is not naive; it is a deliberate choice, a beacon that guides him through uncertainty. It is the fuel that powers his drive for change and serves as the catalyst for his ongoing efforts to improve himself and the world around him.

The chapter emphasizes the importance of maintaining hope as a source of strength and motivation. Amir's journey teaches that hope is a horizon we all can reach, provided we have the courage to chase it, the wisdom to recognize it, and the perseverance to hold onto it, no matter the storms we face.

Upon the canvas where dawn's colors blend,
Amir gazes far, where sea and sky end.
The horizons of hope in his eyes do gleam,
A tapestry woven from his every dream.

With every sunrise, a promise anew,
Skies painted with strokes of a golden hue.
Amir's heart sails towards this radiant light,
Guided by hope, through the darkest night.

The future beckons, a siren's sweet call,
Over the waves, beyond the tempest's squall.
Hope is his anchor, steadfast and sure,
In the ocean of life, it remains pure.

Through storms and calm, he holds hope tight,
A beacon burning, oh so bright.
For hope is the star that never fades,
A lustrous light that never shades.

So let us join Amir on this quest,
With horizons of hope in our chest.
For in the dawn's early, tender scope,
Lies the boundless sea of hope.

Chapter Ten: The Unforeseen Gale

Thrusts Amir into the midst of an unexpected crisis, a metaphorical gale that tests his resolve and adaptability. This chapter explores the sudden and unpredictable challenges that life throws at Amir, forcing him to confront his vulnerabilities and question his preparedness. The gale represents the chaotic forces that can disrupt even the most well-planned journeys, demanding quick thinking and decisive action.

Amir's response to the gale is a testament to his character; he remains steadfast, drawing upon his accumulated wisdom and the strength of his connections to navigate through the turmoil. The narrative emphasizes the importance of resilience and the ability to remain calm in the face of chaos. Amir's experience with the unforeseen gale serves as a reminder that while we cannot control every aspect of our lives, we can control our reactions, turning even the fiercest winds into a chance for growth and learning.

In the heart of calm, where silence reigned,
Amir's world was suddenly unchained.
An unforeseen gale, from the blue it came,
A tempest of fate, wild and untame.

With sails unfurled, he faced the blast,
A test of will, from first to last.
The gale, it roared, a fearsome sound,

But Amir stood firm, he held his ground.

The winds of chance, so fierce and cold,
Could not unseat his grip, his hold.
For in his heart, a fire burned,
With every gust, a lesson learned.

The gale, a teacher, harsh and true,
Showed Amir strength he never knew.
And when the storm had passed on by,
He found new resolve; his spirit high.

So let us face our gales head-on,
From dusk's last star to dawn's first yawn.
For in the winds that we withstand,
We find the strength to take a stand.

Chapter Eleven: The Oceans of Opportunity"

charts Amir's journey as he sets sail across the vast and unpredictable oceans of chance and potential. This chapter captures the essence of Amir's entrepreneurial spirit, highlighting his ability to identify and seize the opportunities that arise in the unpredictable waters of the business world. Amir's ventures are depicted as ships navigating these oceans, each representing a venture that promises new horizons.

His keen eye for untapped markets and innovative ideas serves as his compass, guiding him through uncharted territories. The narrative underscores the significance of being open to new possibilities and the courage required to pursue them. Amir's story illustrates that those opportunities, like oceans, are boundless and bottomless, and the bold harness their currents to reach the shores of success.

The chapter is a testament to the adage that fortune favors the brave, encouraging readers to embark on their own voyages of opportunity.

In the vast expanse where dreams set sail,
Amir's ship embarks, with a hopeful gale.
The oceans of opportunity wide and clear,
Call to the brave, to those who dare to steer.

With a compass of courage in his steady hand,
He charts a course to the promised land.
Where waves of chance crash and roar,
Amir finds paths unseen before.

Each swell of sea, a door to open wide,
To dive into depths where fortunes hide.
The spray of success on his weathered face,
Marks every mile, every challenge he'll embrace.

For Amir knows as he rides each crest,
That seizing the moment is life's grand quest.
The oceans of opportunity, boundless and vast,
Are his to explore, from first to last.

So let us set our sails to the winds of fate,
And journey to where new adventures await.
For in the oceans of opportunity, we find,
The strength to leave the safe harbor behind.

Chapter Twelve: The Waves of Wealth

"Chapter Twelve: The Waves of Wealth" navigates through Amir's encounters with prosperity, likening his financial success to the undulating waves of the ocean.

This chapter delves into Amir's relationship with wealth, portraying it as a force that ebbs and flows with the tides of his endeavors. Amir's acumen in harnessing these waves is central to his narrative, demonstrating how he capitalizes on the crests of opportunity while remaining vigilant during the troughs of economic downturns.
The wealth he accumulates is not an end in itself but a resource for achieving broader goals. Amir's philanthropic efforts and investments in social causes are highlighted, illustrating his belief in the

redistributive power of wealth. The chapter emphasizes the responsibility that comes with financial abundance, showcasing Amir's commitment to using his wealth to create waves of positive change, rather than merely accumulating it for personal gain.

Upon the crests of fortune, Amir rides,
Where the waves of wealth swell high and wide.
A sea of gold, under the sun's bright gaze,
Amir sails through the monetary maze.

The tides of finance rise and fall,
To the siren's call, he gives his all.
With every wave, a lesson learned,
In the fires of commerce, his fortune earned.

The wealth he gathers, not for greed,
But seeds to plant, for those in need.
Amir knows well the ebb and flow,
Of riches reaped from the seeds we sow.

For wealth is like the ocean's might,
It can drown or lift to greater height.
Amir steers clear of the tempest's wrath,
Charting a course on a righteous path.

So let us ride these waves with care,
And share the bounty, fair and square.
For in the waves of wealth, we find,
A chance to leave no one behind.

Chapter Thirteen: The Sea of Solitude

The book delves into the quieter, more introspective moments of Amir's life, where he confronts the solitude that accompanies his journey.

This chapter portrays solitude not as mere isolation but as a vast sea that holds both the weight of loneliness and the freedom of self-discovery. Amir navigates this sea, using the time for reflection and personal growth.

The narrative explores how solitude can be both a challenge and an opportunity, a space where Amir contemplates his past decisions, plans for the future, and reconnects with his inner self.

The sea of solitude becomes a place where Amir faces his fears and doubts, emerging with a clearer sense of purpose and a renewed commitment to his values. The chapter suggests that solitude, much like the sea, is a natural part of life's journey, offering moments of calm and introspection essential for weathering the storms and celebrating the successes ahead.

In the sea of solitude, Amir finds his way,
Where whispers of silence have their say.
The waves of loneliness lap at his soul,
In this ocean vast, he seeks his role.

The waters are still, the depths run deep,
Here, Amir's thoughts to himself, he keeps.
A sea of solitude, a reflective state,
Where he learns to navigate his fate.

Alone with the stars, his only light,
Guiding him through the quiet night.
The sea of solitude, a place to mend,
Where Amir finds peace, an old friend.

In the stillness, he hears life's call,
Echoing in the sea's grand hall.
A place to ponder, to grow, to be,
In the sea of solitude, Amir is free.

So let us sail these silent seas,
And find our strength in the gentle breeze.
For in solitude's embrace, we come to see,
The beauty of our own company.

Chapter Fourteen: The Depths of Desire

explores the profound yearnings that drive Amir's actions and the evolution of his ambitions. Initially, Amir's desires stem from a selfless place, focused on the welfare of his homeland and the betterment of humanity. As he delves deeper into his journey, these desires mature, becoming more nuanced and reflective of his growing understanding of what it means to effect change.

The chapter portrays Amir's desires as a deep ocean, vast and powerful, driving him towards his goals with an unstoppable force. His longing for success is not for fame or fortune but as a means to fulfill his dream of contributing to society.

The narrative reveals how Amir's desires, while personal, are intrinsically linked to the collective good, suggesting that the most profound aspirations transcend individual achievement and resonate with the universal quest for progress.

In the depths of desire, where dreams are born,
Amir's heart sails forth, like a ship in the morn.
With a compass of passion, he charts his way,
Through the waters of want, where the deep sirens play.

His desires, a current, strong, and profound,
Pulling him deeper, where hopes are found.
For the good of his homeland, his heart does yearn,
In the depths of desire, where the fire burns.

Amir's dreams, like treasures, lie on the seabed,
Glimmering with promise, where few dare to tread.
His longing for success, not for fame's sweet kiss,
But to uplift his people, to grant them bliss.

The depths of desire, they call to us all,
To dive into passions, to answer the call.
For in the heart's ocean, so vast and so wide,
Lie the pearls of purpose, in the depths inside.

So let us plunge into these waters so deep,
Where the echoes of our desires, will forever keep.
For in the depths of desire, we find our true quest,
To seek out our dreams and give life our best.

Chapter Fifteen: The Reflections of Regret

This Chapter is a poignant exploration of Amir's introspective journey through the landscape of his past regrets. It reveals Amir's deep-seated remorse over the unexperienced joys of childhood, the superficial familial connections, and the forced departure from his homeland that led to missed final farewells.

These regrets are not mere shadows but formative experiences that profoundly shape Amir's psyche. The narrative delves into how Amir grapples with the sorrow of his children's absence and the unrealized dream of an ideal family.

Despite the pain, Amir learns to navigate these regrets, finding solace in acceptance and the pursuit of new beginnings.

The chapter underscores the universal nature of regret and the possibility of growth it presents. Amir's reflections serve as a reminder that while regret is an inevitable part of life, it can also be a catalyst for change and a deeper understanding of oneself.

In the quiet halls of yesteryear's light,
Amir walks alone, through the day and the night.
With reflections of regret in his weary eyes,
He ponders the past, where truth never dies.

The childhood unplayed, the laughter unsung,
The familial bonds that were never quite strung.
A homeland left behind, not by choice, but by fate,
The funerals missed; the goodbyes too late.

Regret is a shadow that trails Amir's stride,
A silent companion, always by his side.
For the dreams unfulfilled, and the time slipped away,
In the garden of memory, where his thoughts often
stray.

Yet, in the mirror of regret, Amir finds a way,
To learn from the past, to embrace the new day.
For every sorrow, there's a lesson so clear,
In the heartache, there's a love that's so dear.

So let us reflect on the paths we have trod,
On the moments we've lost, on the chances we've shod.
For in the reflections of regret, we can see,
The person we were, and the one we can be.

Chapter Sixteen: The Islands of Innovation

Amir's unwavering belief in the power of innovation is
the cornerstone of his business success. Amir views
innovation not as mere technological advancement but
as a mindset of approaching challenges with unique,
unexpected solutions.

His life story is a testament to this belief, showcasing
how he embraced innovative thinking from an early age
to overcome obstacles and achieve his goals.

The chapter illustrates Amir's conviction that anyone can be an innovator by finding new ways to reach objectives, often through unconventional actions.

It highlights his journey of building a business empire grounded on this principle, where each success story is an 'island' of innovation, contributing to a more extensive archipelago of progress and creativity. Amir's narrative encourages embracing innovation in all aspects of life, reinforcing that it is the key to unlocking potential and driving change.

In the sea of sameness, Amir sought a shore,
Where the sands of the mundane, he'd tread no more.
With a heart full of fire and an inventive mind,
He set sail for the islands of innovation to find.

Each island, a concept, a novel terrain,
Where the fruits of creativity freely reign.
Amir's vessel, his enterprise, cutting through waves,
Past the reefs of repetition, for he's no one's slave.

Innovation, his compass, his guiding star,
Leading him to lands where the thinkers are.
With every idea, a new island in sight,
Amir charts a course through the darkest night.

For him, innovation is not just invention's spark,
But a way to light up the world from the dark.

A method, a process, a unique approach,
To solve the puzzles that life does encroach.

So let us join Amir, in his quest so bold,
To seek out new stories, yet to be told.
For in the islands of innovation, we find,
The treasures of progress for all humankind.

Chapter Seventeen: The Lighthouse of Leadership

Illuminates Amir's journey as a beacon of guidance, embodying the best leadership principles. Amir's leadership philosophy is deeply rooted in service, vision, integrity, and humility. He is portrayed as a lighthouse, providing direction and hope to those within his sphere of influence.

His approach to running his business is characterized by empowering his team, fostering innovation, and making decisions with a blend of analytical and intuitive wisdom. Amir's leadership style is not about commanding from the top but about collaborating and building a culture of mutual respect and support.

The chapter emphasizes Amir's leadership's impact on building a strong, fair reputation and the lasting influence he has on his organization and community. Through Amir's story, the narrative explores the essence of true leadership—inspiring others to find their own path to success and contributing to a collective vision of progress.

Upon the shore, where leaders stand,
Amir's lighthouse casts light across the land.
A beacon of guidance in the darkest night,
A symbol of strength, of foresight, of might.

With a foundation firm in the shifting sands,
Amir's leadership far and wide expands.
Through storms and calm, his light does shine,
A steady presence, both wise and benign.

He guides the lost, the searching, the weary,
His light, a promise that the path is clear, see.
For Amir knows the power of a leader's role,
To illuminate the path, to guide, to console.

In the lighthouse of leadership, Amir stands tall,
A sentinel of progress, heeding the call.
For those who follow, his light is a gift,
Through fog and tempest, it gives them a lift.

So let us learn from Amir's steadfast glow,
To lead with purpose, to let our light show.
For in the lighthouse of leadership, we find,
The way to inspire to uplift humankind.

Chapter Eighteen: The Maps of Morality

Navigates through the ethical landscapes that Amir traverses throughout his career. This chapter underscores the moral principles that serve as Amir's compass, guiding him through complex decisions and interactions.

His unwavering commitment to fairness, honesty, and justice is depicted as a map that he consults at each crossroad, ensuring his path aligns with his core values.

Amir's respect for others, regardless of their age or status, and his innate desire to be helpful, are highlighted as key coordinates on his moral map.

The narrative delves into how Amir's adherence to these principles not only shapes his personal and professional life but also influences those around him, fostering an environment of trust and integrity.

The chapter reflects on the idea that morality is not a destination but a continuous journey, one that requires constant navigation and adjustment to maintain the right course.

In the realm of right, where virtues dwell,
Amir charts his course with a moral swell.
The maps of morality, in his hands unfurled,
Guide him true through a complex world.

With every step, he marks the chart,
With actions kind, straight from the heart.
Fairness is the compass that guides his way,
Through the seas of gray, come night or day.

Honesty's beacon, shining oh so bright,
Cuts through the fog, banishes the night.
Amir's path is clear, his journey just,
In the maps of morality, he places his trust.

Patience, like the tides, ebbs, and flows,
Teaching Amir to wait, as wisdom grows.
Justice, the anchor, holds him fast,
Ensuring his values will forever last.

So let us navigate with Amir's creed,
And in the maps of morality, we'll succeed.
For in the journey of life, we must chart,
A course that reflects the goodness of our heart.

Chapter Nineteen: The Ports of Philanthropy

Details Amir's dedicated shift towards philanthropic endeavors, emphasizing his desire to create a lasting social impact.

This chapter describes Amir's strategic expansion of his charitable efforts, establishing regional chapters worldwide to address educational and humanitarian needs.

Amir's philanthropy is not just about financial contributions; it's a hands-on mission to serve the underprivileged and foster development in the Middle East, Africa, Asia, South America, and in areas of need in Europe.

His commitment to giving back is rooted in a deep sense of gratitude and a recognition of his own blessings.

The narrative portrays Amir's realization that true fulfillment comes from serving others, aligning with his belief that humanity is created to love and support one another.

The chapter concludes with Amir's profound understanding that the essence of life lies in giving, caring, and preparing a better tomorrow through acts of kindness today.

In the ports of philanthropy, Amir's ship does dock,
Where the waves of charity break on the rock.
His cargo is kindness, his treasure is care,
For the people in need, both here and there.

With a heart wide open, like the ocean's expanse,
Amir gives with a spirit that's more than chance.
From the Middle East sands to the jungles so green,
His generosity's felt, though he's seldom seen.

Education and health, his foundation's creed,
Planting the seeds of knowledge like a deed.
For every child in want, every soul in plight,
Amir's ports of philanthropy shine a light.

The chapters of his life, now bound in love,
A legacy written in the stars above.
For in giving we receive, in charity we find,
The truest wealth of humankind.

So let us sail with Amir, across the sea,
To the ports of philanthropy, where we're meant to be.
For in the act of giving, our hearts set sail,
On the noblest voyage, where love prevails.

Chapter Twenty: The Legacy of Learning

Encapsulates Amir's profound dedication to education as the foundation for empowering future generations.

This chapter highlights Amir's belief that knowledge is the cornerstone of progress for both individuals and nations.

Through his foundation, Amir channels his passion for learning into action, providing access to education for countless children in need. His efforts are not limited to building schools; they extend to creating scholarships and mentorship programs that foster a nurturing environment for young minds.

Amir's conviction that education is the key to unlocking potential and achieving development goals is evident in every initiative he undertakes. The narrative celebrates Amir's commitment to spreading enlightenment, suggesting that countries and individuals can realize significant progress through education.

The chapter portrays Amir's legacy as one that will ripple through time, as the seeds of knowledge he plants grow into a forest of wisdom and opportunity.

In the halls of wisdom where echoes resound,
Amir's legacy of learning is profoundly found.
With every book opened, every lesson taught,
A world of enlightenment is eagerly sought.

The legacy he builds, not of stone or of gold,
But of minds awakened, and stories untold.
For knowledge is a treasure that forever gives,
In the hearts of the young, where it truly lives.

From the desks of the needy to the chairs of the keen,
Amir's vision of education is clearly seen.
A beacon of hope in a world so vast,
His legacy of learning is unsurpassed.

For he knows the power that knowledge can wield,
In the classroom, the field, or the academic field.
A legacy not just for the present day,
But a gift for tomorrow, come what may.

So let us join Amir, in this noble quest,
To teach, to learn, to give our best.
For in the legacy of learning, we all play a part,
In the timeless journey of the educated heart.

Chapter Twenty-One: The Harbor of Humanity

This chapter is the culmination of Amir's life's work, where he anchors his legacy in the acts of kindness and progress that define his existence. In this final chapter, Amir makes a monumental decision to donate most of his wealth to charitable causes, focusing on education and expanding his foundation's global reach.

His retirement is not an end, but a new beginning, as he dedicates his time and resources to establishing regional chapters that serve as harbors of hope and assistance for the needy across various continents. Amir's actions are driven by a profound sense of gratitude and a desire to give back to the world that has given him so much.

The chapter reflects on Amir's realization that life's purpose is found in love, generosity, and the care we extend to others. It is a powerful testament to the belief that we are created to make a positive impact, and that our legacy is measured by the lives we touch and the future we help shape.

In the harbor of humanity, Amir casts his net,
Spreading kindness wider than the sunset.
With a heart so vast, and a vision so grand,
He reaches out with a generous hand.

Eighty percent of wealth, he gives away,
To charity, to education, come what may.
His life's twilight, not for rest or play,
But to serve, to uplift, in every way.

From the Middle East's sands to South America's sun,
His chapters of giving have just begun.
A legacy of love, for the young and the old,
More precious than silver, more lasting than gold.

Amir's final chapter, on life's great sea,
Is a testament to what one man can be.
For in giving, we live, and in living we give,
In the harbor of humanity, where all can truly live.

So let us sail with Amir, to the end of our days,
In the harbor of humanity, where love always stays.
For in the act of giving, our souls are set free,
In the harbor of humanity, where we're meant to be.

PART THREE

Harmony's Odyssey: Earth's Journey

Harmony's Odyssey: Earth's Journey

Galactic Poem

In the vast tapestry of the cosmos, where stars are born and galaxies dance to the universe's rhythm, lies our humble abode, Earth. This anthology of poems, "Harmony's Odyssey: Earth's Journey," embarks upon a narrative that transcends the boundaries of time and space. It delves into the heart of our planet's struggles and triumphs, reflecting the delicate balance between humans and nature.

As we stand at a pivotal moment in history, this anthology offers not just a reflection but a call to action. Through the verses of "Galactic Poems," we traverse the landscapes of Earth, witnessing its beauty and fragility. Each poem serves as a beacon, guiding us through the tempestuous storms of our own making towards the calm harbors of hope and unity.

The journey begins with Chapter 1: The Gathering Storm, which exposes the environmental and societal crises facing Earth. These verses are not merely words on a page; they are echoes of humanity's collective conscience, urging us to heed the warnings and embrace the wisdom that can restore balance.

Through the lens of the United Galaxies Council, we gain a broader perspective on our actions and their repercussions, reminding us that we are but one part of a much larger cosmic community.

As you turn these pages, let the poetry resonate with your spirit. Let it inspire you to look beyond the immediate and the mundane and see the interconnectedness of all life. May it stir within you a sense of responsibility and a desire to contribute to the healing of our world.

"Harmony's Odyssey" is not just an anthology of poems; it is a journey of the soul. It is an invitation to sail towards a future where humanity lives in harmony with itself and with the universe. So let us embark on this odyssey together, with hearts open to the possibilities of what we can achieve when we come together in love and unity.

Chapter by chapter, this anthology will take you through the critical moments of Earth's odyssey..

Let us find our way in the harbor of humanity, where love always stays. For in the act of giving, our souls are set free; in this freedom, we rediscover our proper place in the cosmos.

Welcome to "Harmony's Odyssey: Earth's Journey."
May this voyage through words and emotions light your
path and fill your heart with hope.

Chapter 1: The Gathering Storm

In Chapter 1: The Gathering Storm, a crisis is looming
on Earth due to unsustainable practices and
environmental neglect.

The planet's ecosystems are on the brink of collapse,
and society is plagued by inequality and unrest. Despite
advancements in technology and knowledge, humanity
struggles to address these challenges.

The United Galaxies Council (UGC), an interstellar
alliance, observes Earth's predicament with concern.
The chapter sets the stage for Earth's journey from the
brink of disaster towards a sustainable and harmonious
future.

In the heart of the night, where whispers lay,

A storm was born, at the break of day.

It brewed in silence, it brewed so deep,

In the cradle of the sky, where comets sleep.

The clouds amassed, a formidable sight,

A tapestry of gray, blocking the light.

The wind it howled, a mournful tune,

As if it mourned for the absent moon.

The sea roared back, with waves so high,

Reaching for the storm, up in the sky.

The dance was fierce, the dance was long,

Nature's forces, both mighty and strong.

The trees did bend, the leaves did fly,

As the storm declared its battle cry.

The earth it trembled, the mountains stood,

Witness to the storm, in the ancient wood.

The lightning struck, a brilliant lance,

Illuminating the storm's wild dance.

The thunder roared, an echo vast,

A sound to remember, long after it's passed.

And in the midst, where fear might dwell,

A gathering of souls, their stories to tell.

They stood as one, against the gale,

Their spirits unbroken, they would not fail.

For in the storm, they found their might,

In the heart of darkness, they found the light.

Together they stood, as the storm unfurled,

A band of hearts, against the world.

So let the storm come, let it rage on,

For when it passes, a new day is born.

And in its wake, the world will see,

The power of unity, the strength of the free.

Chapter 2: Earth's Echo

In Chapter 2: Earth's Echo, Earth's deteriorating condition sends out a metaphorical 'echo' across the cosmos, reaching the United Galaxies

Council (UGC). The UGC, an interstellar alliance, is deeply concerned about Earth's environmental crisis and societal unrest.

They contemplate extending their help, but are also wary of intervening in Earth's affairs without invitation. The chapter highlights the UGC's dilemma and sets the stage for potential interstellar intervention in Earth's future

In the wake of the storm, the silence speaks,

A whisper of earth, through valleys and peaks.

The echo of life, a subtle sound,

In the heart of the wild, where wonders abound.

Harmony listens, to the earth's soft call,

The rustle of leaves, in the autumn's fall.

The murmur of streams, over pebbles they glide,

A melody pure, in nature's stride.

The roots of the trees, like fingers entwine,

Grasping the essence, of the divine.

The soil's rich scent, a comforting balm,

In the world's great palm, a tranquil calm.

The birds they sing, a chorus so bright,

A symphony of joy, from morning till night.

Each note an echo, from the earth's deep core,

A song of a planet, of lore and more.

Harmony feels, the pulse of the land,

The beat of the earth, beneath her hand.

The rhythm of life, so vast and so wide,

In every heartbeat, she feels the tide.

The mountains echo, with ancient might,

Standing as sentinels, in the fading light.

Their peaks like notes, on a stave so high,

Composing the music of the sky.

The dance of the shadows, with the light's embrace,

A delicate balance, a tender chase.

Harmony's journey, through shadow and gleam,

Is a dance with the earth, a living dream.

For every echo, from the earth that springs,

Is a reflection of life, and the hope it brings.

And Harmony's path, on this earthly plane,

Is an echo of love, again and again.

So let the earth speak, let its voice be heard,

In the flutter of wings, in the call of a bird.

For in its echo, the truth is found,

And in its rhythm, we are all bound.

Chapter 3: The Fractured Accord

In Chapter 3: The Fractured Accord, the United Galaxies Council (UGC) grapples with internal disagreements over intervening in Earth's crisis. While some members advocate for direct intervention, others argue for non-interference in Earth's affairs.

The chapter highlights the complexities of interstellar diplomacy and the challenges of reaching a consensus in the face of divergent ideologies and interests. The 'Fractured Accord' signifies the discord within the

UGC, setting the stage for future deliberations on Earth's fate.

In the realm where light and shadow blend,

A fracture forms, a beginning and an end.

The accord once whole, now split in twain,

On Harmony's odyssey, in sun and rain.

The whispers of unity, now but a dream,

As the accord dissolves, like a forgotten theme.

The pieces lie scattered, a puzzle undone,

A tapestry unraveled, its threads come undone.

Harmony seeks, through the fractured shards,

For the melody lost, in the broken bards.

The notes that once soared, in a perfect chord,

Now silent, in the wake of the accord.

The earth it quakes, with a silent plea,

For the harmony lost, for the unity to be.

The sky it weeps, with a mournful tear,

For the accord that broke, in the face of fear.

Yet in the cracks, where the light seeps through,

A glimmer of hope, in the morning dew.

The chance to mend, what was torn apart,

With the needle of courage, and the thread of heart

.

Harmony walks, on a path unsure,

With a resolve so strong, and a spirit pure.

She gathers the pieces, with tender care,

A mission of healing, a breath of air.

For every fracture, a chance to heal,

For every sorrow, a chance to feel.

And in the journey, through the shadow's gate,

Lies the power to mend, and to recreate.

So let the accord break, let it fall to the ground,

For in its breaking, a new path is found.

And Harmony's odyssey, through fracture and form,

Is a testament to strength, in the heart of the storm.

Chapter 4: Earth's Ultimatum

In Chapter 4: Earth Ultimatum, the United Galaxies Council (UGC) reaches a critical decision point. Recognizing the severity of Earth's environmental crisis and societal unrest, the UGC issues an ultimatum to Earth's leaders. They are given a choice to accept the UGC's assistance and commit to a path of sustainability and harmony, or face the dire consequences of their actions alone. The chapter underscores the urgency of Earth's situation and the pivotal role of the UGC's intervention in shaping Earth's future.

Upon a world, where balance sways,

An ultimatum, in the sun's fierce rays.

The earth it speaks, with a voice so grave,

A demand for respect, for the brave to save.

The rivers run, with a message clear,

Flowing with purpose, for all to hear.

The oceans surge, with a mighty claim,

An ultimatum, in nature's name.

Harmony stands, at the crossroad's edge,
A pledge in her heart, a solemn pledge.
To heed the call, of the earth's command,
To honor the life, of the sea and land.

The forests whisper, with leaves that shake,
A warning of loss, for humanity's sake.
The mountains echo, with a stone-cold truth,
An ultimatum, for the old and youth.

The sky it darkens, with a storm's return,
A lesson unlearned, is a lesson to burn.
The earth it quakes, with a righteous roar,
An ultimatum, not heard before.

Harmony feels, the weight of the world,
In her hands, the future unfurled.
A choice to make, a path to tread,
For on her journey, the earth has led.

The ultimatum, a call to action,

For every deed, a chain reaction.

And Harmony's odyssey, on this earthly sphere,

Is a quest for balance, far and near.

So let the earth speak, let its voice ring true,

For its ultimatum, is a call to renew.

And in Harmony's steps, with each stride and turn,

Is the hope that the world, will listen and learn.

Chapter 5: The Galactic Standoff

In Chapter 5: The Galactic Standoff, the United Galaxies Council's (UGC) ultimatum to Earth leads to a tense standoff. Earth's leaders, grappling with the prospect of interstellar intervention, are divided on their response. While some see the UGC's offer as a lifeline, others view it as an infringement on Earth's sovereignty.

The chapter highlights the complexities of Earth's decision-making process and the geopolitical implications of the UGC's ultimatum. The 'Galactic

Standoff' signifies the tension between Earth and the UGC, setting the stage for future developments.

In the cosmos vast, where silence reigns,

A standoff stirs, in celestial domains.

Stars align in a tense array,

On Harmony's odyssey, in night and day.

Galaxies spin, a slow, grand dance,

As two forces meet, in a cosmic chance.

A standoff of light, a standoff of dark,

A balance of power, in the universe's arc.

Harmony gazes, into the void,

Where peace and war, are both employed.

The planets they watch, with bated breath,

As the standoff unfolds, in life and death.

The comets they streak, with tails so bright,

Carrying messages, through the endless night.

A silent witness, to the grand affair,

The galactic standoff, in the open air.

The black holes whisper, of power untold,

Of secrets kept, in their folds so old.

The standoff echoes, in their dark embrace,

A game of shadows, in the cosmic space.

Harmony's heart, beats with the stars,

Feeling the tension, of the cosmic wars.

A journey of wonder, a journey of might,

In the galactic standoff, between shadow and light.

The nebulae bloom, like flowers in space,

A backdrop of beauty, to the standoff's grace.

A canvas of color, in the dark expanse,

Setting the stage, for the cosmic dance.

And in the standoff, where fates collide,

Harmony finds, where her truths reside.

For in the vastness, of the starlit dome,

She understands, the universe is home.

So let the galaxies, their standoff hold,

For in their story, the future's told.

And Harmony's odyssey, through space so grand,

Is a voyage of discovery, in the galaxy's hand.

Chapter 6: Earth's Rebellion

In Chapter 6: Earth Rebellion, the United Galaxies Council's (UGC) ultimatum sparks a rebellion on Earth. A faction of Earth's leaders, opposed to UGC's intervention, rallies public support and instigates a global uprising.

They reject the UGC's offer, asserting Earth's sovereignty and the right to determine their own fate.

The rebellion signifies a significant turning point, escalating the tension between Earth and the UGC, and setting the stage for a potential interstellar conflict. The chapter underscores the complexities of interstellar diplomacy and the struggle for autonomy in the face of a global crisis.

In the cosmos' vast expanse, a fleet draws nigh,

With Earth in sight, under the watchful sky.

A rebellion stirs, the people's cry,

Under Terra's Shield, they'll live or die.

Dr. Luna Marez, voice of the free,

Declares, "No tyranny of stars shall we see.

United, our Earth, in fierce decree,

For self-determination, we'll forever be."

From city sprawl to fields of green,

The spirit of Terra has never been more keen.

With every soul, the movement's seen,

A declaration of will, pure and serene.

In shadows deep, the networks weave,

Connecting minds that dare to believe.

Against Guardians' tech, they plot and conceive,

With hackers in tow, they'll not be deceived.

Dr. Marez, with fervor, leads the fray,
"Show the UGC we're not astray.
A sovereign world, in bright array,
Governing ourselves, come what may.

The Guardians approach, with might and main,
But Earth's defenses cannot constrain.
Electromagnetic shields, a forceful bane,
And swarming drones, their advance detain.

Xylo-Thorax, in council's seat,
Questions if their actions were too concrete.
"Have we pushed them too far in our conceit?
Their determination, none can defeat."

On Earth, a unity begins to form,
Dissolving lines of the norm.
A renaissance from the storm,
In science, culture, a new transform.

As the ultimatum's hour draws near,
Earth stands united, without fear.
The Guardians face a sphere,
Armored by will, the message clear.

Dr. Marez, in historic plea,
Addresses all, for the galaxy to see.
"A crossroads here, for you and me,
Recognize our sovereignty, let us be."

The UGC ponders Earth's fate,
A rebellion's force they did not anticipate.
The decision's weight, they deliberate,
But Earth's resolve, it's too late to abate.

So ends the chapter, with Earth's might,
A planet that stands, ready to fight.
The future uncertain, but burning bright,
For Terra's Shield, in the endless night.

Chapter 7: The Siege of Earth

In Chapter 7, the Earth faces an unprecedented threat as alien forces besiege the planet. Humanity, caught off guard by the sudden attack, scrambles to mount a defense. Amidst chaos, heroes emerge, leading a desperate fightback against the invaders.

The chapter vividly describes the battle's intensity, the defenders' courage, and the civilians' plight. As the siege continues, Earth's forces suffer heavy losses, but their resolve remains unbroken. The chapter ends on a cliffhanger, with Earth's fate hanging in the balance, awaiting the outcome of this epic struggle for survival.

The Ballad of the Siege

Upon the blue orb's armored shore,

The Guardian fleet did fiercely roar.

Earth's sentinels, in the void so stark,

Unleashed their fury, a celestial arc.

Xylo-Thorax, with dread, did gaze,

As conflict bloomed in a fiery blaze.

"Not this path," he cried with a plea,

"Seek we peace, or lost we'll be."

A clash of wills, not merely of might,

Guardians and Earthlings in a plight.

Ideals at war, in the cosmic night,

Each seeking to prove their own right.

In secret conclave, away from the fray,

Earth's envoys with UGC did parley.

A summit proposed, on lunar clay,

To halt the siege and find a way.

Xylo-Thorax, with hope anew,

Agreed to meet 'neath the sky so blue.

"The cosmos vast, for me and you,

Let's coexist, as peaceful folk do."

On the Moon, they gathered 'round,

With Earth behind, a sight profound.

Negotiations tense, as stakes did mount,

Each side's plea, they did recount.

Earth's leaders firm, with sovereign call,

While UGC sought order for all.

A young voice rose, above the squall,

"A beacon of hope, we shall install."

Her vision clear, of a future bright,

A planet healed, in the galaxy's sight.

Moved were they, by her guiding light,

Seeing Earth anew, a hopeful knight.

The siege lifted, not by force,

But words and vows set a new course.

Earth transformed, with no remorse,

A leader in sustainability's discourse.

The defenses fell, the fleet withdrew,

The skies cleared, a peaceful view.

The Siege of Earth, in history's hue,

A lesson learned, of what understanding can do.

Remembered not as a violent storm,

But a turning point, a new norm.

Where harmony's path was finally worn,

In understanding and cooperation, reborn.

Chapter 8: The Path to Peace

Chapter 8: The Path to Peace describes a pivotal moment in Earth's history. Following a prolonged siege by the Guardian fleet, Earth and the United Galaxies Council (UGC) engage in tense negotiations on the Moon. The discussions are fraught with challenges as both sides present their demands. Earth's leaders advocate for autonomy and respect for sovereignty, while the UGC insists on compliance with environmental regulations.

A breakthrough occurs when a young Earth delegate proposes a vision for Earth's future, emphasizing sustainable living as a model for the galaxy. This vision moves the UGC delegates, who begin to see Earth not as a rogue planet but as a beacon of hope.

The siege ends not with conflict but with dialogue and promises. The UGC agrees to lift the siege, and Earth pledges to lead by example in transforming its industries and societies to be sustainable and environmentally conscious.

The chapter concludes with dismantling Earth's orbital defenses and the departure of the Guardian fleet. The skies are clear once more, symbolizing the absence of ships and weapons and the fear and uncertainty that had gripped the planet. The Siege of Earth is remembered as a turning point towards harmony and cooperation.

The Anthem of Harmonia

For days, the siege held, a relentless tide,

Neither Earth nor Guardians would abide.

Yet in the tumult, a silent stride,

A movement for peace, they could not hide.

In secret chambers, away from the fray,

Earth's stewards and UGC found a way.

A pact was formed, to end dismay,

Project Harmonia would lead the day.

The Guardians receded, Terra's Shield at rest,

A battered Earth, yet its spirit unbested.

Together they ventured on a quest,

For cooperation, respect, a mutual zest.

Towers of purity pierced the skies,

Cleansing the air, where hope lies.

Oceans teemed, as drones arise,

Healing the waters under watchful eyes.

Forests returned, deserts in bloom,

Green cities soared, dispelling gloom.

Space debris vanished, giving room,

For starry paths, and safety's boon.

Society transformed, a sustainable core,

Green jobs flourished, pollution no more.

Education reformed, to the very floor,

Diplomacy, stewardship, became the lore.

Guardians, once feared, now friends in kind,

Shared wisdom, guidance, for humankind.

Dr. Marez, with a future aligned,

Spoke of unity, a shared mind.

The Earth-UGC summit, a grand affair,

On a healed Earth, fresh and fair.

A celebration, a solemn swear,

To continue the work, with tender care.

The Path to Peace, more than a tale,

A new history written, without fail.

A testament to cooperation, a hearty hail,

To the enduring spirit, that will prevail.

Chapter 9: The Reconciliation

Chapter 9: The Reconciliation details the aftermath of the siege on Earth, focusing on the efforts to rebuild trust between Earth and the United Galaxies Council (UGC). The chapter highlights the initiatives under the 'Intergalactic Restoration Initiative' (IRI), which aims to repair the damage to Earth's environment and infrastructure.

Key points in the chapter include:

Xylo-Thorax's Leadership: Xylo-Thorax, the leader of the UGC, extends an olive branch to Earth, emphasizing the need to overcome past conflicts and work towards a peaceful future.

IRI's Multi-Phased Approach: The IRI is a comprehensive plan with multiple phases, including immediate aid and long-term sustainability projects. Medical and engineering teams are deployed to the most affected areas to provide aid and begin reconstruction.

Ecological Restoration: The second phase of the IRI focuses on ecological restoration, with teams of biologists and ecologists from Earth and the UGC working together to revitalize damaged ecosystems.

Cultural Exchange and Education: The third phase involves education and cultural exchange, with the establishment of interstellar exchange programs to foster learning and understanding between Earth and other civilizations.

Earth's Transformation: Due to these efforts, Earth begins to transform, with cities becoming greener, air and oceans cleaner, and society more united.

Xylo-Thorax's Reflection: Xylo-Thorax reflects on the journey and Earth's resilience, recognizing the unity achieved through reconciliation.

Celebration of 'Day of Reconciliation': The chapter concludes with the celebration of the first 'Day of Reconciliation,' marking the peace forged between Earth and the UGC and the commitment to a united galaxy.

The chapter portrays a new era of unity and cooperation, sparked by recognizing Earth's sovereignty and the shared responsibility for environmental stewardship. It's a testament to the power of reconciliation and the potential for a harmonious interstellar community.

The Verse of Unity

Post siege, the Earth and stars align,

A task of trust, to intertwine.

The scars of war, a stark design,

A reminder of the cost, a line.

Xylo-Thorax, with branch in hand,

Spoke of unity, a future grand.

"Defined not by conflict's brand,

But by our will to together stand.

The Intergalactic Restoration, a plan so wide,

To mend the Earth, side by side.

A multi-phase journey, a stride,

For recovery and sustainability, as guide.

With care, the wounded were treated,

And psychological scars, defeated.

Advanced tech, so warmly greeted,

In hospitals, where hope was seated.

Engineers, a diverse crew,

Worked with Earth's own, to renew.

Knowledge shared, as friendships grew,

A resilient world, they did construe.

Ecological revival, phase two's theme,

Teams united, a shared dream.

Ecosystems healed, a vibrant stream,

Native species returned, a gleam.

The 'Great Green Wall,' ambition's seed,

Against desert sands, a green deed.

Jobs created, communities freed,

A belt of life, from desolation, lead.

Phase three, a cultural weave,

Education, exchange, a reprieve.

From galaxy's wisdom, to conceive,

And Earth's rich tales, to believe.

As the initiative thrived, Earth's face changed,

Greener cities, air cleansed, rearranged.

Oceans alive, the damage estranged,

Innovation and cooperation, exchanged.

Xylo-Thorax, in assembly's light,

Spoke of unity, a future bright.

"From despair's tide, to hope's height,

Together we soar, to unite."

The 'Day of Reconciliation,' a time to reflect,

A galactic holiday, to connect.

Peace and commitment, we select,

A united galaxy, we project.

Chapter 10: Terra's Renaissance

The chapter "Terra's Renaissance" expands to depict Earth's transformation into a beacon of sustainability and innovation. The International Restoration Initiative (IRI) not only rejuvenates the planet but also ignites a global metamorphosis. Cities, once smog-filled, now thrive as hubs of green technology, with lush rooftop gardens and clean, efficient public transport. The Green Canopy satellites, Earth's vigilant sentinels, ensure environmental compliance, symbolizing a new era of stewardship.

Education is reimagined, with curricula emphasizing environmental science and galactic awareness, nurturing a generation poised to inherit a healthier world. The arts, reflecting Earth's resurgence, inspire a cultural renaissance celebrating the symbiosis of technology and nature.

Economically, the green revolution propels job creation, with startups transforming waste into wealth. Terra's Shield, former rebels, now champion sustainability, leading community initiatives to diminish humanity's ecological footprint.

The UGC recognizes Earth's exemplary turnaround and promotes it as a model for ecological recovery. Delegations from across the stars arrive, eager to replicate Earth's blueprint for harmony between civilization and nature.

A grand galactic ceremony marks the culmination of Earth's efforts. Broadcast universally, it showcases verdant landscapes and pristine waters. Dr. Luna Marez, once a dissident, now stands as a testament to the power of unity and innovation, her words resonating with hope.

The inauguration of the Terra Institute of Galactic Studies signifies Earth's ascension as a galactic vanguard, guiding others towards a peaceful coexistence with their environments. This institute, a nexus of learning and research, is dedicated to fostering interstellar relations

and environmental guardianship, ensuring Earth's legacy as a leader in the cosmic community.

The Ode to Terra's New Dawn

With open arms, the Earth did greet,

The IRI's touch, a feat so sweet.

A catalyst for minds to meet,

Innovation's march, not to retreat.

Terra's Shield, from rebels to peacekeepers' role,
With UGC, they forged a whole.
'The Green Canopy,' satellites' patrol,
Monitoring Earth, a vigilant scroll.

The renaissance, a surge of mind and hand,
Creativity and tech across the land.
The Green Canopy, a guardian grand,
A symbol of a future, sustainably planned.

Cities transformed, an urban bloom,
Gardens on roofs, vertical farms consume.
Clean energy transit, giving room,
For skies of blue, and nature's perfume

.

Education reformed, a curriculum wide,
With environmental science as a guide.
Children learned of galaxies beside,
Earth's place in cosmos, with pride.

The arts, a reflection of Earth's revival,

Music and literature, a new survival.

Visual arts, a cultural tidal,

Festivals of unity, a joyful arrival.

Green industries, a boom of chance,

Innovators thrived, in the economic dance.

Startups launched, in a sustainable stance,

Turning waste to resource, in advance.

Terra's Shield, now advocates of care,

Teaching sustainability, everywhere.

Community projects, a breath of fresh air,

Reducing footprints, with flair.

The UGC, by Earth's turnaround impressed,

Used it as a lesson, for the rest.

Delegations learned, on a quest,

To take back knowledge, from Earth's test.

A grand ceremony, Earth's transformation hailed,

Broadcasted wide, as projects sailed.

Lush landscapes, waters, and skies unveiled,

A planet healed, where once it ailed.

Dr. Luna Marez, a leader of progress' wave,

Spoke of a phoenix, from conflict's grave.

"Terra's Renaissance," she said, "will save,

As a beacon of hope, for the brave."

The 'Terra Institute of Galactic Studies,' a new start,

For learning and research, to impart.

Interstellar relations, an art,

Earth, a leader, in the galactic chart.

Chapter 11: The Cosmic Symposium

Chapter 11: The Cosmic Symposium details a historic event where delegates from Earth and representatives of the United Galaxies Council (UGC) gather on the

Moon to negotiate and discuss the future of interstellar environmental policy. The setting, against the backdrop of Earth in the sky, serves as a poignant reminder of what's at stake.

Key points in the chapter include:

Tense Negotiations: Both sides present their grievances and demands, with Earth arguing for autonomy and the UGC emphasizing the need for environmental regulations.

Cultural Exchange: Earth's delegates share their planet's rich cultural heritage while experiencing the diverse cultures of the UGC.

The Marsland Declaration: A document outlining the commitment of all present to uphold the Intergalactic Restoration Initiative (IRI) principles, calling for ongoing cooperation and the establishment of a permanent environmental task force.

Historic Event: The summit on the Moon is seen as a turning point, potentially shaping the future of not just Earth but the interstellar community.

The chapter concludes with a sense of unity and a renewed commitment to a harmonious interstellar society. It highlights the importance of cooperation and mutual respect in addressing environmental challenges. The Cosmic Symposium becomes a symbol of hope and a pledge to continue the work that lies ahead for a sustainable future.

The Ballad of the Cosmic Conclave

On Marsland's plains, 'neath crystal dome,

The Cosmic Symposium found its home.

Delegates gathered, from star to star,

To chart a course for peace, not war.

Dr. Luna Marez, Earth's chosen voice,

Spoke of unity, a collective choice.

"From discord's ashes, we've soared above,

Let this symposium be a sign of our love."

The Crystal Halls, with walls so clear,

Gave view to Mars, and cosmos near.

A reminder vast, of shared space,

A universe we all embrace.

Workshops, panels, discussions round,

On terraforming, ethics sound.

The Green Canopy's tale was told,

A network of care, a future bold.

Engineers shared their storied fight,

To guard the Earth, and set things right.

A live display, data streamed,

Earth's recovery, as they had dreamed.

Dr. Marez, with words so keen,

Told of Earth, once sick, now serene.

"Our planet's a charge, to keep green,

The IRI's start, but more to glean."

A cultural exchange, a symposium's heart,

Music, art, cuisine—a chart.

Earth's heritage, a galaxy's part,

Diverse cultures, a new start.

The 'Marsland Declaration,' a pact to keep,

A commitment strong, not shallow, not cheap.

Cooperation, knowledge, a leap,

An environmental task force, not to sleep.

As stars twinkled, the symposium's end,

A garden of soils, a message to send.

A united front, we all defend,

Environmental challenges, we'll mend

.

Dr. Marez, in contemplation deep,

Gazed at the garden, a promise to keep.

"A microcosm, our universe's sweep,

May it thrive, as our bonds leap."

Chapter 12: The Legacy of Marsland

The Marsland Accord's signing heralded a new epoch, birthing the United Planetary Fund (UPF) to aid environmentally stricken planets. This fund, a crucible of innovation, supported diverse projects, from atmospheric cleansing to wildlife preservation. The Accord itself, a comprehensive environmental treaty, laid down sustainable development guidelines and disaster response frameworks.

The Accord's legacy shone in rejuvenated ecosystems, clean skies, and safeguarded biodiversity. The New Era, marked by the UGC's transformation from authority to mentor, fostered a galactic community cherishing life and planetary health. Education embraced the Accord's history, instilling environmental stewardship in the young.

The Green Canopy satellites, Earth's vigilant guardians, now monitor planetary well-being, symbolizing human ingenuity and

commitment to cosmic safeguarding. Celebrating the Accord's anniversary, the UGC hosted a galaxy-wide festival, planting the 'Garden of Worlds' on Marsland— a testament to diversity and peace.

The 'Cosmic Conservatory' emerged, dedicated to preserving endangered species and ecosystems across the galaxy. Despite challenges, the UGC, Earth, and its allies stood united, their shared history lighting the way. The Marsland Accord's legacy, a beacon of hope and unity, continued to inspire and guide the galactic community towards a sustainable future.

The Epic of Marsland's Legacy

In the annals of time, the Accord was penned,

A beacon of hope, on which worlds would depend.

The United Planetary Fund, a promise extended,

To heal struggling planets, their fates amended.

The UPF, more than a trove of gold,

A nexus of progress, of visions bold.

From skies purified to lifeforms old,

It funded dreams, and stories untold.

The Marsland Accord, a treaty vast,

Sustainable futures, it forecast.

Guidelines for growth, a sustainable cast,

And rapid aid, for disasters amassed.

The legacy lived, in ecosystems thrived,

On barren worlds, now revived.

Skies of clarity, where smog had dived,

Biodiversity's tapestry, artfully contrived.

Epilogue: A New Era, expanded wide,

The UGC's image, now turned aside.

From authority to unity, a source of pride,

The Green Canopy, progress and preservation's guide.

A galactic community, life's sanctity revered,

The UGC mentored, as civilizations steered.

Towards harmony with nature, as they endeared,

A balance of existence, lovingly engineered.

Education systems, with new core themes,

Marsland's history, and Earth's dreams.

Children learned of environmental regimes,

And the web of life, in cosmic streams.

The Green Canopy, once defense, now sight,

The galaxy's guardian, in the cosmic night.

Monitoring health, with data's light,

A testament to our guardianship's might.

The New Era's dawn, with festivals bright,

The Marsland Accord's anniversary, a delight.

A time for reflection, for gratitude's flight,

For principles shared, for unity's height.

The 'Garden of Worlds,' a botanical blend,

Flora from galaxies, a message to send.

Diversity's beauty, peace to extend,

A symbol of unity, that we all defend.

Marsland's legacy, an endless inspiration,

The 'Cosmic Conservatory,' a preservation.

Species and ecosystems, a dedication,

Across the stars, a conservation.

Challenges met, with lessons of old,

The UGC, Earth, a story retold.

United they stand, with resolve bold,

A shared history, a future to mold.

Chapter 13: The Crystal Secrets of Marsland

Marsland's crystal forests, born from a comet's essence, are a cosmic enigma. The crystals resonate with universal frequencies and are believed to encode the secrets of time and space. The UGC's Marsland Observatory and the Keepers of Kaelum, guardians of these forests, collaborate to decipher the crystals' messages.

The crystals' ability to resonate with natural frequencies suggests they hold knowledge of cosmic events. The UGC and the Keepers' symbiotic relationship combines science and mysticism, leading to advancements in interstellar communication.

The Crystal Conclave, a summit of galactic intellects, aims to unlock the secrets of the crystals. A breakthrough by Keeper Lyra reveals the

crystals as active cosmic observers, capable of visualizing distant galaxies.

Marsland's crystals promise universal discovery, positioning the UGC at the vanguard of a cosmic renaissance. The Keepers speak of a 'Lattice of Light,' an empathic energy network connecting the crystals, responsive to sentient emotions.

The UGC's research into this lattice led to the 'Resonance Interface,' which enables direct dialogue with the crystals. This development unveils the crystals as living libraries, holding profound implications for understanding the universe's mysteries. Marsland stands as a beacon of potential, its crystal secrets poised to illuminate the cosmos.

The Ballad of Marsland's Crystals

In Marsland's groves, where crystals rise,

A forest of wisdom beneath the skies.

Towering flora, radiant, wise,

Holding secrets where the comet lies.

Kaelum's Tear, through cosmos soared,

A celestial wanderer, knowledge stored.

Upon Marsland, life it poured,

Seeding enlightenment, forever adored.

Harmonic Crystals, resonance pure,

Vibrations of the universe, an allure.

Scholars and sages, in conjecture,

Seeking patterns, a cosmic lecture.

The Keepers of Kaelum, monks of old,

Guardians of forests, secrets bold.

Crystals sentient, stories told,

A living library, a lore enfold.

Science and mysticism, hand in hand,
Data streams within crystal bands.
Astrophysical truths, a discovery grand,
Navigating stars, a breakthrough planned.

The Crystal Conclave, minds unite,
To unlock secrets, bring to light.
Knowledge for all, a future bright,
Marsland's promise, a guiding kite.

Lyra, the Keeper, a revelation shared,
A distant galaxy, through resonance bared.
Crystals observing, as if they cared,
A universe watched, a vision declared.

The Promise of Marsland, a future foreseen,
A cosmic renaissance, a knowledge demesne.
The UGC, in discovery's sheen,
With Marsland's crystals, a wisdom gene.

The Lattice of Light, a network alive,

Connecting crystals, making them thrive.

Emotions and thoughts, in which they dive,

A web of consciousness, where empathy derives.

The Resonance Interface, a dialogue begun,

With crystals conversing, under the sun.

Questions and answers, a union spun,

Patterns of light, a cosmic run.

The Hearthstone's pulse, a unity call,

A beacon of knowledge, for one and all.

The secrets of cosmos, no longer small,

Illuminating paths, on which we'll never fall.

Chapter 14: The Prophecy Unveiled

Chapter 14, "The Prophecy Unveiled," narrates the Crystal Conclave's discovery of a prophecy within Marsland's crystal forests. Lyra, a Keeper, reveals a vision of Earth's dual futures: one flourishing in harmony, the other a cautionary wasteland. The prophecy shows a bifurcated path, urging the choice of a brighter destiny.

The Galactic Guardians vow to shepherd Earth towards this luminous future, inspiring a global awakening. "The Pathfinders" movement arises, committed to ecological restoration and sustainable progress. A celestial alignment amplifies this transformative energy, marking a decisive moment for Earth.

The United Galaxies Council's "Pledge of the Cosmos" supports Earth's journey, as the prophecy becomes a guiding light for collective

action. Initiatives for reforestation, pollution reduction, and clean energy adoption are launched, with the Guardians offering technological aid.

The impending celestial event symbolizes hope, celebrated as a galactic holiday. Observatories are built, and Earth's people unite, poised to embrace stewardship of the galaxy or face decline.

The chapter concludes with Earth's resolve to follow the prophecy's path, bolstered by the Guardians' support and establishing the 'Galactic Environmental Corps,' ready to address ecological challenges galaxy-wide. The prophecy is a pivotal beacon, guiding Earth's choices and the galaxy's future.

The Saga of the Unveiled Prophecy

In Marsland's embrace, where secrets dwell,

The Crystal Conclave heard the prophecy's tell.

Lyra, the Keeper, with a touch so light,

Awakened the crystal, and with it, foresight.

A vision of Earth, in futures twain,

One of harmony, one of pain.

A paradise reborn, or a barren bane,

The prophecy clear, a dual lane.

The Forked Path, a choice to make,

One of light, one of ache.

Verdant trees or barren flake,

Earth's destiny, at stake.

Guardians of the galaxy, once stern,

Now protectors, with concern.

Guiding Earth, at every turn,

For the bright future, they yearn.

Earth's Awakening, a slumber's end,

The Pathfinders' journey, they wend.

Following light, the path they bend,

Towards a future, they intend.

The Celestial Alignment, a cosmic sign,

Planets in harmony, a design divine.

Energies of change, intertwine,

A pivotal moment, a chance to shine.

The Pledge of the Cosmos, a declaration,

A call to all, for Earth's salvation.

Support and witness, a new foundation,

For a dawning era, a celebration.

Epilogue: The Choice of Ages,

A beacon for endeavors, as history's pages.

The celestial event, as it stages,

Uniting Earth, as it engages.

The Pathfinders' initiatives, a plan so bold,

Reforestation, clean energy, a future foretold.

The Guardians' aid, technologies unfold,

A Galactic Environmental Corps, in the mold.

The alignment nears, a symbol of hope,

Observatories watch, a telescopic scope.

A galactic holiday, a universal trope,

On Earth, united dreams elope.

As planets align, a wave cascades,

Over Earth, a transformation parades.

Atmosphere clear, life upgrades,

A protector's role, Earth persuades.

The Festival of the Alignment, a joyous day,

On Earth and Marsland, a bright array.

Lights, music, a new way,

The prophecy fulfilled, by those who sway.

Chapter 15: The Dawning of the Celestial Event

Chapter 15: The Dawning of the Celestial Event encapsulates a transformative period for Earth as it approaches a significant celestial alignment. This event is anticipated to have profound effects on Earth and across the cosmos. Here's a summary of the chapter:

The Pathfinders: A group of visionaries and activists known as the Pathfinders works to align Earth's future with a prophesied celestial event, inspiring hope among the once doubtful masses.

Natural Phenomena: Earth itself begins to show signs of awakening, with dormant natural phenomena coming to life, symbolizing the planet's response to the upcoming alignment.

Harmonic Convergence: The celestial alignment is depicted as more than an astronomical event; it's a convergence that

Resonates with the soul of the universe, heralding new beginnings.

Marsland's Crystals: On Marsland, crystal forests resonate with frequencies related to the alignment, suggesting that they not only reveal Earth's potential future but also actively participate in its realization.

Galactic Embrace: The United Galaxies Council declares a day of meditation and reflection, with civilizations across the stars focusing their collective consciousness on Earth.

Unity and Revelation: As the alignment peaks, Earth experiences a profound sense of unity and revelation, with the Marsland crystals casting beams that infuse Earth's atmosphere with the potential for change.

The Celestial Accord: Following the alignment, Earth's leaders and the Pathfinders unveil new guidelines for a sustainable way of life, balancing technological advancement with environmental stewardship.

The Age of Harmony: The chapter concludes with the beginning of the Age of Harmony, marking Earth's transformation into a testament to the power of unity and collective action.

The chapter paints a picture of a pivotal moment in Earth's history, where the collective efforts of its people and the cosmic influence of the celestial event lead to a harmonious and prosperous future. Earth emerges as a beacon of hope and an integral member of the galactic community, ready to embrace its destiny among the stars.

The narrative emphasizes the importance of unity, cooperation, and every individual's role in shaping the future. Earth's new path is celebrated globally, with the celestial alignment leaving a lasting impact on the planet and its inhabitants.

The Rhapsody of the Celestial Dawn

As planets dance and stars align,

The Earth's rebirth, a sign divine.

The Pathfinders' dream, a design,

To weave a future, bright and fine.

The Awakening of Terra, a world anew,

Nature's chorus, a vibrant hue.

Geysers' joy, auroras' view,

Skies of hope, in morning dew.

The Harmonic Convergence, a cosmic song,

Planets' symphony, where we belong.

A melody of beginnings, strong,

A universe's soul, to which we throng.

The Crystal Catalyst, Marsland's heart,

Forests hum, a frequency's art.

Keepers chant, their sacred part,

Prophecy's moment, set to start.

The Galactic Embrace, a mindful pause,

Council's decree, for a noble cause.

Civilizations unite, without flaws,

Supporting Earth, with cosmic applause.

The Turning Tide, a breath as one,

The Day of Alignment, under the sun.

Unity's sense, not to be undone,

A step into the future, begun.

The Crystal Revelation, a light so bold,

Marsland's beams, a story told.

Earth infused, a change to mold,

A connection to cosmos, to behold.

The Path Forward, The Celestial Accord,

A sustainable life, in harmony's chord.

Technology and nature, in concord,

A prophecy's promise, aboard.

Epilogue: The Age of Harmony's rise,

A testament to unity, Earth's prize.

A collective will, under the skies,

A better world, before our eyes.

The Pathfinders' wind, a cosmic whisper,

Of change, of thriving, of a galactic sister.

A message of a time, to muster,

A community of stars, to cluster.

The Keepers' ritual, an ancient tone,
Amplifying energy, through crystal stone.
A Galactic Embrace, a reflection zone,
Emissaries of knowledge, Earth's loan.

The Turning Tide, a wave to generations,
The Day of Alignment, spirits' elevations.
A celestial dance, across nations,
A role for all, in Earth's narrations.

The Crystal Revelation, a deeper wake,
A role for each, in Earth's remake.
The beams' touch, for every stake,
Hearts and minds, the crystals take.

The Path Forward, a new constitution,
A promise of beauty, a resolution.
The Age of Harmony, a celebration,
Monuments of commitment, a foundation.

A scene of Earth, a gem so bright,

Lights of unity, a peaceful night.

The celestial alignment, a past flight,

An Age of Harmony, in sight.

Chapter 16: The Legacy of the Alignment

Chapter 16: The Legacy of the Alignment reflects on a celestial event's profound and lasting impact that marked the beginning of a new era for Earth. Here's a summary of the chapter:

• The Green Revolution: Earth experiences a surge in sustainable living and clean energy, leading to cities becoming eco-friendly ecosystems.

• Crystal Technology Exchange: The Keepers of Kaelum share the secrets of Marsland crystals, leading to technological advancements on Earth.

• Intergalactic Alliance: Earth joins the United Galaxies Council's Intergalactic Alliance, emphasizing its commitment to cosmic stewardship.

• Guardians' New Mission: The Galactic Guardians transform into the Guardians of Harmony, focusing on peace and ecological balance.

• Cultural Renaissance: Earth sees a cultural revival, with arts and music inspired by the cosmos, fostering a sense of unity across civilizations.

• Cosmic Voyage: Humanity embarks on the Harmony Expedition, exploring distant worlds and symbolizing Earth's role as a learner in the galaxy.

• Prophecy's Continuation: The Marsland crystals continue to offer insights, hinting at an era of enlightenment spreading across the galaxies.

• Harmonic Epoch: The Age of Harmony evolves into the Harmonic Epoch, with Earth's journey becoming a key chapter in galactic history.

• Eco-Architects' Rise: Visionaries design self-sustaining buildings that contribute to the planet's health and create standalone ecosystems.

• Alliance's Expansion: The Intergalactic Alliance addresses social and economic disparities, aiming for a thriving galaxy for all beings.

• Guardians' Missions: The Guardians of Harmony undertake missions to restore worlds and prevent conflicts, symbolizing hope and assistance.

• Cultural Impact: Earth's cultural renaissance significantly impacts the galaxy, with the Interstellar Art Festival becoming a celebrated event.

- Exploration Age: The Harmony Expedition leads to further space exploration, focusing on understanding and learning from the cosmos.

- New Prophecy: A new prophecy suggests a future where barriers between worlds dissolve, leading to a higher consciousness in the galaxy.

- Era of Growth: The Harmonic Epoch is characterized by growth and enlightenment, with the galaxy becoming more connected and conscious.

The chapter concludes with a panoramic view of Earth, now a beacon of harmony in the cosmic sea, its influence continuing to shape its destiny and that of its inhabitants. The celestial alignment's legacy is a testament to the power of change and unity. Earth's transformation inspires a harmonious future in the galaxy.

The Legacy of the Alignment: An Epic Verse

The alignment's past, its legacy unfurled,

A new epoch on Earth, in the cosmic world.

The Age of Harmony, a future pearled,

With groundbreaking leaps, a flag unfurled.

The Green Revolution, a wildfire spread,

Clean energy, sustainable life, ahead.

Cities bloomed, ecosystems wed,

Skyscrapers with gardens, a green thread.

The Crystal Technology Exchange, a pact made,

Marsland's secrets, in Earth's aid.

Communication, energy, a new blade,

Crystal tech, in life's parade.

The Intergalactic Alliance, a coalition born,

Earth as a member, a new dawn.

Preservation, advancement, a cosmic sworn,

An interstellar stewardship, adorned.

The Guardians' New Mission, peace to keep,

Ecological balance, a watchful sweep.

Aid to planets, a nurturing leap,

Guardians of Harmony, a promise deep.

The Cultural Renaissance, arts in bloom,
Inspired by stars, beyond Earth's room.
Music, literature, a cultural plume,
Galactic unity, dispelling gloom.

The Cosmic Voyage, humanity's dream,
Harmony Expedition, a starry beam.
Exploring, learning, a galactic theme,
Not conquerors, but learners, supreme.

The Prophecy's Continuation, crystals tell,
Insights of cosmos, a ringing bell.
A new era of enlightenment, a swell,
With Earth as beacon, a story to spell.

The Harmonic Epoch, centuries' song,
From destruction's brink, to unity strong.
A pivotal chapter, where we belong,
The alignment's echo, lifelong.

Eco-Architects rise, visionaries' plan,
Reshaping landscapes, a new clan.
Self-sustaining buildings, a lifespan,
Solar skins, turbines, a water can.

The Crystal Tech, a cornerstone's role,
Devices powered, efficiency's goal.
Everyday life, a crystal bowl,
Surpassing means, a conventional shoal.

The Alliance's strength, Earth's crucial part,
Social, economic gaps to outsmart.
A galaxy thriving, a united heart,
Opportunity for all, a new start.

Guardians of Harmony, missions of old,
Restoring worlds, stories bold.
Symbols of hope, a future told,
Assistance promised, a hand to hold.

Cultural Renaissance, a galaxy's effet,

Earth's art and music, a cultural sect.

Interstellar Art Festival, a project,

Participants from cosmos, to connect.

The Harmony Expedition, a path paved,

A new age of exploration, craved.

Journeys of discovery, a way waved,

Knowledge returned, a galaxy saved.

A prophecy of barriers, dissolved away,

A consciousness rising, a spiritual fray.

Understanding, empathy, a new day,

A galaxy connected, in every way.

The Harmonic Epoch, not just peace,

Growth, enlightenment, never cease.

Connected, conscious, a release,

A galaxy more united, a masterpiece.

A panoramic Earth, a vibrant view,

Oceans blue, lands green, a hue.

The alignment's memory, a guiding clue,

A beacon of harmony, forever true.

Chapter 17: The Galactic Response to Earth's

A galaxy connected, in every way

Chapter 17: The Galactic Response to Earth's Metamorphosis details the widespread impact of Earth's transformation into a beacon of sustainability and harmony. Here's a summary of the chapter:

• Galactic Milestone: Earth's Age of Harmony inspires civilizations across the galaxies, marking a significant milestone in galactic history.

• Zephyrians' Enlightenment: The Zephyrians, initially skeptical, are humbled by Earth's resurgence and seek to exchange knowledge on ecological balance.

• Andromedans' Alliance: Led by President Xylo-Thorax, the Andromedans invite Earth to join the

Andromedan Consortium for cultural and technological exchange.

• Sirians' Sympathy: Moved by Earth's dedication to ocean revival, the Sirians initiate the 'Blue Bonds' project to protect aquatic ecosystems galaxy-wide.

• Centaurians' Collaboration: Known for advanced agriculture, the Centaurians share sustainable farming techniques with Earth, enhancing food security.

• Orion's Overture: The Orions collaborate with Earth's architects to construct eco-cities in the Orion Belt that can sustainably accommodate billions.

• Pleiadians' Peace: The Pleiadians embrace Earth's cultural renaissance and propose 'Harmonic Convergence Festivals' to celebrate unity and diversity.

• Vega's Vision: Inspired by Earth's satellites, the Vegans suggest the 'Stellar Network' to monitor planetary health across the Milky Way.

• Cosmic Congregation: Earth's transformation catalyzes a new era of cooperation, with the United Galaxies Council evolving into a unified congregation.

The chapter concludes with a view of the Milky Way as a tapestry of interconnected civilizations. Earth actively participates in the cosmic dance, showcasing the power of unity and change. The narrative emphasizes the collaborative efforts and shared vision for a sustainable future among the stars. Earth's metamorphosis becomes a testament to the strength of unity and the potential for positive change on a galactic scale. The chapter portrays a universe where cooperation and wisdom lead to prosperity and peace for all life forms.

The Harmonic Epoch, not just peace,

Growth, enlightenment, never cease.

Connected, conscious, a release,

A galaxy more united, a masterpiece.

A panoramic Earth, a vibrant view,

Oceans blue, lands green, a hue.

The alignment's memory, a guiding clue,

A beacon of harmony, forever true.

The Galactic Response: A Celestial Verse

When Earth's rebirth sent ripples wide,

The cosmos watched with open-eyed.

The Age of Harmony, Earth's pride,

A galactic milestone, side by side.

The Zephyrians' Enlightenment, a respect new-found,

Their gaseous forms, with admiration crowned.

Emissaries to Earth, knowledge unbound,

Atmospheric secrets, a common ground.

The Andromedans' Alliance, a hand extended,

Earth's culture and tech, beautifully blended.

In the Consortium, a partnership splendid,

Art and exploration, horizons amended.

The Sirians' Sympathy, oceans deep,

'Blue Bonds' project, a conservation leap.

Aquatic life, a promise to keep,

Galaxy-wide protection, a bond to reap.

The Centaurians' Collaboration, agriculture shared,

Sustainable farming, resources spared.

Food security, for all prepared,

A green harvest, by all cared.

The Orion's Overture, an architectural feat,

Eco-cities with Earth, a mission complete.

Billions housed, a triumph neat,

Environment unharmed, a task discrete.

The Pleiadians' Peace, a cultural embrace,

Harmonic Convergence Festivals, a galactic grace.

Unity and diversity, in a cosmic space,

Earth's journey, a peaceful base.

The Vega's Vision, satellites to weave,

A Stellar Network, the Vegans conceive.

Planetary health, a web to achieve,

Monitoring and maintenance, to relieve.

Epilogue: The Cosmic Congregation, a unity spun,

A new era of cooperation, under the sun.

The Council evolved, a vision begun,

A harmonious universe, not to be undone.

The Zephyr Exchange, a program to flow,
Atmospheric tech, a mutual glow.
Renewable energy, Earth's show,
For Zephyrians' cities, a power to stow.

The Andromedan Consortium, a melting pot,
Earth's fresh perspective, a cultural plot.
Art and science, a deeper thought,
Understanding fostered, a gap fought.

The 'Blue Bonds' project, a conservation model,
Sirians and Earthlings, in water they toddle.
New courses charted, a protective coddle,
Aquatic life ensured, a vital bottle.

The Green Harvest Initiative, a revolution in food,
Centaurian and Earthly methods, a sustainable mood.
Feeding billions, a planetary brood,
Natural resources, forever renewed.

The Orion Belt, with new cities risen,

Sustainability and ecology, a shared vision.

Earth's collaboration, a precise incision,

Harmony with nature, a final decision.

The Harmonic Convergence Festivals, a cultural norm,

Peace talks and relations, a galactic form.

Earth's harmony, a guiding storm,

Inspiring worlds, to peacefully transform.

The Stellar Network, a Vegan's dream,

Expanding Earth's Canopy, a satellite beam.

Monitoring health, a planetary theme,

Swift responses, a united team.

The Cosmic Congregation, a chapter anew,

The Council, with Earth, a unity to view.

Voices from stars, a wisdom to pursue,

Alliance and prosperity, for the many, not few.

A panoramic Milky Way, a tapestry bright,

Worlds and civilizations, in shared light.

Earth, a vibrant participant, a sight,

Its metamorphosis, a cosmic might.

Chapter 18: The Shadow Stirring

Chapter 18: The Shadow Stirring outlines the emergence of a rogue faction known as the Eclipse Syndicate in the Andromeda Galaxy. Discontent with the prevailing peace, they seek to reignite chaos and conflict, believing it to be essential for evolution and innovation. Here's a summary of the chapter:

• Eclipse Syndicate's Ideology: The Syndicate, comprising dissidents and radicals, believes that strength is born from adversity and views the galactic harmony as stagnation.

• Covert Operations: They initiate covert operations to destabilize peace, spreading propaganda and inciting unrest without revealing their presence.

• Guardians' Dilemma: The Guardians of Harmony must adapt to this new invisible threat that challenges the light of harmony they are sworn to protect.

• Council's Response: The United Galaxies Council holds an emergency session to devise a strategy that maintains unity while countering the Syndicate's threat.

• Silent War: The Star Sentinels work to dismantle the Syndicate's schemes, maintaining peace while engaging in a silent war against the faction.

• Turning Point: The Syndicate's attempt to corrupt the Marsland crystals is thwarted by the Keepers of Kaelum and the Star Sentinels, leading to the Syndicate's exposure and downfall.

•   Eclipse's End: The Syndicate leaders are offered a choice between joining the harmonious society or exile.

• Harmony Preserved: The Syndicate's fall reinforces the need for active peace maintenance and the importance of vigilance and resolve to sustain harmony.

The chapter concludes with a reflection on the Syndicate's impact, emphasizing that while their belief in the necessity of adversity holds some truth, their methods were flawed. The galactic community's firm stance against the ideological assault and the Guardians' role as beacons of hope highlight the collective strength in overcoming challenges. The legacy of the celestial alignment and the Syndicate's shadow serve as reminders of the value of harmony, guiding the galaxies towards a brighter future. The chapter portrays a galaxy that, despite facing the shadows of conflict, remains united and stronger than ever.

The Shadow Stirring: A Galactic Rhythm

In Andromeda's depths, a shadow was cast,

The Eclipse Syndicate, from the past.

Discontent with peace, they amassed,

Yearning for chaos, their die was cast.

The Syndicate's Creed, adversity's fire,

Strength forged in conflict, their desire.

Galactic harmony, they did conspire,

To disrupt and challenge, to inspire.

The Disruption Begins, a covert thread,

Propaganda, unrest, a sense of dread.

Sabotage in silence, a fear widespread,

The Syndicate's presence, subtly spread.

The Guardians' Dilemma, a new foe,

An invisible enemy, a hidden woe.

Defenders of light, against a shadow,

A mission to protect the harmony's glow.

The Council's Response, a session called,

A threat rising, their unity appalled.

A confrontation avoided, peace installed,

A different approach, the Syndicate stalled.

The Silent War, in cosmos' shade,

Star Sentinels' countermeasures made.

Dismantling schemes, a silent crusade,

Preserving peace, a facade displayed.

The Turning Point, the crystals' call,

The Keepers alerted, to prevent a fall.

A mission to protect, to stand tall,

Exposing the Syndicate, once and for all.

The Eclipse's End, a mission true,

Leaders captured, their plots in view.

A choice offered, to start anew,

Join harmony or to the fringes, withdrew.

Epilogue: The Harmony Preserved,

A reminder that peace must be served.

Vigilance and resolve, never swerved,

The Age of Harmony, rightly deserved.

The Syndicate's creed, a symbol now,

Of misguided ambition, a broken vow.

Ideological disruptions, they did plow,

But the galactic community, firm in its bow.

The Guardians of Hope, a beacon bright,

Strength in protection, not in fight.

Adapting to shadows, with all their might,

A commitment to peace, day and night.

The Council's healing, a strategic play,
Against discord's seeds, a mindful fray.
Reconciliation, not retribution's way,
Healing the rifts, come what may.

The Silent War, a cosmic feel,
Star Sentinels' actions, the peace they seal.
Covert yet crucial, with zeal,
Preserving society, the common weal.

The Turning Point, unity's stand,
Against the Syndicate, hand in hand.
The crystals' sanctity, a demand,
A new beginning, a future grand.

The Eclipse's end, a galaxy's rise,
A new chapter, under the skies.
Redemption's path, a wise prize,
Harmony's principles, the Syndicate defies.

The Epilogue's lesson, a vigilance keen,

Mindfulness eternal, a peaceful scene.

The shadow's edge, always seen,

Moving forward, together, serene.

A renewed purpose, stars align,

The Age of Harmony, ever divine.

The celestial legacy, a sign,

Harmony treasured, forever shine.

Chapter 19: The Unseen Wisdom

Chapter 19: The Unseen Wisdom explores the aftermath of the Eclipse Syndicate's fall and the introspection it prompts across the galaxies. The key points of the chapter are:

• Reexamination of Ideology: The Syndicate's belief in conflict as a catalyst for evolution raises questions about progress and the role of adversity, leading the Council to form a committee to explore these ideas.

• **Doctrine of Dualities:** The committee develops the Doctrine of Dualities, recognizing the need for balance between harmony and discord for true progress.

• **Galactic Challenges:** To honor the Syndicate's unintended legacy, the Council establishes the Galactic Challenges, peaceful competitions to stimulate innovation and resilience.

• **Guardians' New Role:** The Guardians of Harmony oversee the Galactic Challenges, ensuring they promote unity.

• **Syndicate's Rebirth:** The remnants of the Syndicate are offered a chance to join the new initiative or remain in exile, with many choosing redemption.

• **Harmonic Balance:** The galaxies thrive under the Doctrine of Dualities, with civilizations engaging in the Galactic Challenges and fostering a dynamic society.

• **Crystal Confluence:** The Marsland crystals resonate with a new frequency that speaks of balance and growth.

• **Symphony of the Stars:** The galaxies dance to the Symphony of the Stars, celebrating the duality of existence and entering an Era of Dynamic Equilibrium.

The chapter concludes with a vision of the future where the Symphony of the Stars resonates in every being, and the galaxies move together in a grand cosmic ballet, reflecting the wisdom of both light and shadow. The narrative emphasizes the importance of balance, unity, and the collective journey towards enlightenment.

The Unseen Wisdom: A Rhythmic Ode to the Cosmos

In the aftermath of shadow's fall,

The galaxies pondered the Syndicate's call.

A kernel of truth, in darkness' thrall,

The unseen wisdom, behind it all.

The Ideology Reexamined, a conflict's role,

Evolution's catalyst, a challenging toll.

The Council's quest, to understand the whole,

Seeking wisdom in the Syndicate's soul.

The Doctrine of Dualities, a balance sought,

Harmony and discord, a philosophical thought.

True progress in equilibrium, caught,

Too much of either, a lesson taught.

The Syndicate's Legacy, unintended yet true,

Challenges and growth, a perspective anew.

Galactic Challenges, a peaceful venue,

Stimulating innovation, without conflict's hue.

The Guardians' New Quest, a role embraced,

Overseeing challenges, integrity laced.

Competition united, not displaced,

A spirit of unity, intergalactically traced.

The Rebirth of the Syndicate, a choice to make,

Redemption's path, a new life to partake.

Constructive challenges, for progress' sake,

Champions of advancement, a future to wake.

The Harmonic Balance, galaxies thrive,

Science, art, philosophy, alive.

A dynamic society, destined to strive,

Under dualities' doctrine, they contrive.

The Crystal Confluence, a frequency born,

Neither harmony nor conflict, but a balance adorned.

Marsland's crystals, in cosmic shifts, sworn,

A melody of growth, in the cosmos, worn.

Epilogue: The Symphony of the Stars,

A cosmic composition, healing scars.

The Age of Harmony, reaching far,

Into an Era of Dynamic Equilibrium, no bars.

The Doctrine of Dualities, a philosophy deep,

In schools taught, in minds a leap.

Adversity's measure, a powerful sweep,

In advancement's quest, a climb steep.

The Galactic Challenges, a tradition's flame,

Debates, exhibitions, a celebrated name.

Broadcast inspiration, a camaraderie game,

Diverse civilizations, in innovation's aim.

The Guardians of Harmony, a purpose found,

Mentors, facilitators, in challenges wound.

Healthy competition, in spirit sound,

Guiding participants, to success bound.

The Syndicate's rebirth, a redemption's tale,

From undermining peace, to its strongest scale.

A transformation, a new trail,

The Council's wisdom, in choice, prevail.

The Harmonic Balance, prosperity's era,

Civilizations flourish, a harmonious terra.

Ideas exchanged, a resource's chimera,

Societies reaching heights, an ecological sera.

The Crystal Confluence, cosmic knowledge's key,

Complex patterns unraveled, a universe's decree.

Keepers and scientists, in discovery's spree,

Nature's forces understood, a cosmic sea.

The Symphony of the Stars, an enlightened age's song,

A melody of existence, where we all belong.

The dance of planets, the pulse of stars, strong,

A fabric of reality, harmonizing along.

The Era of Dynamic Equilibrium, a profound mark,

Growth and stability, in light and dark.

Galaxies embracing change, a harmonious arc,

Guided by harmony, through the ages, stark.

A vision of the future, where stars resonate,

Galaxies in ballet, wisdom to celebrate.

The Symphony of the Stars, a cosmic fate,

In every being's heart, it does not abate.

Chapter 20: The Redemption Quest

• **Journey Commences:** Cipher and the Harmony Brigade face challenges that reflect the Syndicate's ideology, forcing Cipher to confront his past.

• **Trials of Redemption:** The deeper they go, the more complex the trials become, testing their perceptions, logic, and resilience against echoes of time.

• **Heart of the Maze:** At the labyrinth's heart, Cipher realizes the true challenge is understanding the Orb's purpose, which reflects unity rather than power.

• **Orb's Revelation:** Cipher discovers that the labyrinth tests harmony, not intellect or strength.

• **The Return:** Transformed by the Orb's wisdom, Cipher and the Brigade return with a message of unity and cooperation.

• **Epilogue:** Cipher's quest becomes legendary, symbolizing that redemption is possible through unity. The chapter concludes with Cipher, transformed from a harbinger of discord to a beacon of light, standing before the Council. His journey signifies a new era of understanding and unity, with the galaxies looking towards a future shaped by past lessons. Cipher's quest has altered the course of history, emphasizing that wisdom and unity are the strongest forces in the galaxy.

The narrative highlights the power of redemption and the collective strength found in facing challenges together. Earth and the galaxies stand at the dawn of a new era, inspired by Cipher's transformation and the Symphony of Redemption.

The Redemption Quest: A Rhythmic Chronicle

From shadows deep, Cipher arose,

A quest for redemption, to oppose.

The architect of chaos, now proposes,

A journey through time, the Labyrinth encloses.

Cipher's Pledge, a maze to brave,

The Labyrinth of Infinity, a path to pave.

The Orb of Unity, at its heart to save,

A cosmic trial, for the bold and grave.

The Council's Deliberation, a team to form,

Harmony Brigade, through the storm.

A quest for good, a pledge to transform,

Cipher's journey, a unity norm.

The Labyrinth's Legacy, an ancient test,

A trial of worthiness, for those who quest.

Puzzles of life, a cosmic zest,

The Syndicate's past, in Cipher's chest.

The Journey Commences, knowledge in hand,

Through quantum puzzles, a life's demand.

Astrophysics, essence of land,

Trials reflecting, a past to remand.

The Trials of Redemption, illusions faced,

Perceptions tested; logic displaced.

Echoes of time, in loops encased,

A deeper labyrinth intricately laced.

The Heart of the Maze, the Orb in sight,

Pulsating with cosmos, a powerful light.

Cipher's realization, in the Orb's might,

Harmony's test, not strength or fight.

The Orb's Revelation, a mirror's role,

Reflecting unity, a collective soul.

Not power over cosmos, but a harmonious toll,

The labyrinth's purpose, to make whole.

The Return, with wisdom's seed,

Cipher and Brigade, from the maze freed.

A message to the Council, a united creed,

Strength in many, a common need.

Epilogue: The Symphony Resonates,

A legend told, across starry states.

Redemption's reminder, unity creates,

A path from darkness, to light's gates.

Cipher's Transformation, a soul's voyage,

From harbinger of discord, to concord's assemblage.

A testament to change, a past's camouflage,

The Harmony Brigade, a respect's homage.

The Labyrinth's Lessons, a spirit's forge,

In trials' fires, their unity gorge.

Puzzles and paradoxes, a future's forge,

Closer to each other, to the Orb's verge.

The Echoes of Time, not just a barrier,

Reflections of futures, a temporal carrier.

Choices made, history's librarian,

The Brigade's actions, a continuum's clarion

.

The Orb's Custodians, guardians anew,

A symbol of wisdom, a shared view.

The Orb's power, not to subdue,

But to share, a wisdom true.

The Council's Evolution, a beacon's light,
Guiding civilizations, through dark to bright.
Cipher's journey, a guiding kite,
A beacon of enlightenment, a council's might.

The Symphony of Redemption, a melody's play,
Across the stars, a harmonious way.
Courage, change, a will to sway,
The power of redemption, in cosmic array.

The Dawn of Understanding, a new era's birth,
Shadows of past, lessons of worth.
Wisdom's currency, unity's girth,
A future bright, for the galaxy's hearth.

Cipher, once shadow, now light's beam,
Before the Council, a fellowship's dream.
Eyes of warmth, a fellowship's gleam,
A quest that changed, the cosmic stream

Chapter 21: The Echoes of the Labyrinth

Chapter 21: The Echoes of the Labyrinth describes the profound connection between Earth's ecosystems and the cosmic journey of Cipher and the Harmony Brigade through the Labyrinth of Infinity. Here's a summary of the chapter:

• Resonance with Earth: As the Brigade navigates the labyrinth, Earth's natural environments begin to resonate with their trials, suggesting a cosmic connection.

• Whispering Forests: Earth's forests mirror the labyrinth's puzzles, showing bursts of growth and vitality that reflect the Brigade's progress.

• Singing Oceans: The oceans respond to the Brigade's challenges, with new currents forming and marine life flourishing in sync with the labyrinth's energy.

• Dancing Deserts: Deserts come to life, revealing hidden oases and blooming cacti as Cipher and the Brigade unlock survival secrets.

• **Soaring Skies:** Birds trace celestial paths in the sky, reflecting the clarity of thought achieved within the labyrinth.

• **Vigilant Mountains:** Mountains echo the Brigade's strength and endurance, with rock formations symbolizing the trials faced.

• **Resonant Ice:** Polar ice caps resonate with the labyrinth's essence, stabilizing and feeding rivers and lakes.

• **Orb's Influence:** The Orb of Unity amplifies Earth's response, enhancing the symbiotic relationships between species and their environments. • **Epilogue – The Living Labyrinth:** Earth becomes a living labyrinth, a testament to the power of unity and diversity, with ecosystems flourishing as a mirror to the harmony achieved by the Brigade.

The chapter concludes with Earth transformed by the echoes of the labyrinth, its inhabitants inspired to create and innovate, and the planet itself growing in complexity and beauty. The narrative emphasizes the interconnectedness of all life and the transformative power of unity, with Earth standing as a testament to the symphony of life that resonates across its verdant fields and within the hearts of its people. The journey through the Labyrinth of Infinity has left a lasting impact, inspiring future generations and contributing to Earth's ecological renaissance. Earth, now a living labyrinth, is a dynamic and ever-adapting testament to the power of unity and the strength found in diversity. The chapter portrays Earth as a flourishing world, echoing the harmony achieved by Cipher and the Harmony Brigade in their quest for redemption.

The Echoes of the Labyrinth: A Rhythmic Poem

In the vastness of space, a labyrinth lies,

Its echoes reach Earth, under cosmic skies.

Cipher and the Brigade, with unified ties,

Navigate its maze, where wisdom defies.

The Whispering Forests, leaves in converse,

Rustling with puzzles, the labyrinth's verse.

Challenges mirrored, a growth so diverse,

Trees intertwine, the maze's paths traverse.

The Singing Oceans, harmonies deep,

Riddles of fluid, the tides' leap.

New currents cleanse, marine life's sweep,

Synchronized movements, the labyrinth's keep.

The Dancing Deserts, life's embrace,

Sands shift, revealing an oasis's grace.

Cacti bloom, colors inter lace

Creatures revel, in abundance's space.

The Soaring Skies, birds in flight,

Tracing paths celestial, a majestic sight.

Atmosphere clears, air alight,

Clarity of thought, the labyrinth's might.

The Vigilant Mountains, peaks aspire,

Echoing resolve, challenges transpire.

Rock formations shift, natural spires,

Monuments to trials, the labyrinth's fire.

The Resonant Ice, whispers of change,

Glaciers stabilize, rivers arrange.

The ice speaks, a balance's range,

Lessons of permanence, the labyrinth's exchange

.

The Orb's Influence, Earth's response,

Energy pulses, symbiosis ensconced.

Ecosystems evolve, resilience pronounced,

Interconnected growth, by the Orb announced.

Epilogue: The Living Labyrinth, Earth's rebirth,

Challenges catalyst, ecological mirth.

A testament to unity, diversity's worth,

Flourishing ecosystems, a mirror of mirth.

The Echoes of the Labyrinth, consciousness touch,

Dreams of patterns, inspiration's clutch.

Creating, innovating, problems' crutch,

The labyrinth's influence, a guiding hutch.

The Dreaming Jungles, vines entwine,

Flowers bloom, cosmic design.

Wildlife adapts, in the labyrinth's line,

Thriving in change, a natural sign

.

The Murmuring Plains, tales they sway,

Grasses in rhythm, herds' ballet.

Mimicking the maze, a painted display,

The labyrinth's story, in the plains' relay.

The Orb's Echo, across Earth's sphere,

Waves of energy, unity's cheer.

Collaboration inspired, cultures endear,

The Orb's harmony, nations revere.

The Harmony Brigade's Legacy, heroes' return,

Lessons of the labyrinth, for all to learn.

A symbol of potential, adversity's spurn,

Unity's narrative, a collective yearn.

The Labyrinth's Continuum, mythology's part,

Inspiring generations, a challenging art.

The Living Labyrinth's Growth, a dynamic chart,

Complexity and beauty, the labyrinth's heart.

Earth stands testament, unity's power,

The Echoes of the Labyrinth, life's bower.

A symphony played, in every hour,

Across verdant fields, a life's shower.

Chapter 22: The Fork in the Cosmic Road

Chapter 22: The Fork in the Cosmic Road delves into the profound implications of choices made within the Labyrinth of Infinity and their resonating effects across the cosmos. Here's a summary of the chapter:

• **Cosmic Consequences:** The chapter emphasizes that every decision has far-reaching consequences, shaping the destiny of individuals, civilizations, and galaxies.

• **Path of Light:** Earth's choice of the path of light leads to growth and harmony, inspiring other civilizations and fostering innovation through the Galactic Challenges.

• **Path of Shadows:** The alternative path of shadows, representing chaos and power, is shown as a potential route that could have led to discord and isolation.

• **Ripple Effect:** Choices create ripples affecting not only the immediate environment but also distant worlds and future generations.

• **Universal Tapestry:** The cosmos is likened to a tapestry woven from decisions, with the labyrinth's trials reflecting the cosmic dance of choices and consequences.

• **Doctrine of Dualities:** This philosophy acknowledges the value of both harmony and adversity, advocating for a balance between the two.

• **Echoes of Marsland:** The Marsland crystals capture the echoes of these paths, singing of the path of light's beauty and cautioning against the path of shadows.

• **Guardians' Vigil:** The Guardians of Harmony stand vigilant, guiding civilizations towards the light and offering counsel against the temptations of the shadows.

• Cosmic Crossroads: The chapter concludes with the universe at a crossroads, where civilizations hold the power to choose their path, shaping the fabric of reality.

The narrative underscores the importance of balance, unity, and collective wisdom in navigating the cosmic road. It portrays a universe where the choices of its inhabitants are interwoven into an ever-changing, ever-growing tapestry, leading to infinite possibilities and a shared heritage that unites the stars.

The chapter reflects on the impact of decisions and the importance of maintaining harmony and vigilance in the face of potential adversity. The cosmos is depicted as a living entity pulsating with its inhabitants' choices, and the paths of light and shadows are intertwined, creating a road that leads to infinite possibilities.

The chapter concludes with a vision of the cosmos as a living entity pulsating with its inhabitants' choices. The paths of light and shadows intertwined, creating an ever-changing, ever-growing road, a cosmic road that led to infinite possibilities.

The Fork in the Cosmic Road: A Poetic Journey

In the labyrinth's heart, a truth profound,

Choices made, a cosmic sound.

Paths of light and shadows bound,

Through the universe, they resound.

The Path of Light, a beacon's call,

An era of growth, a rise from fall.

Inspiring galaxies, one and all,

Galactic Challenges, a unity ball.

The Path of Shadows, a dire route,

Chaos and power, the Syndicate's shout.

Discord's balance, fear and doubt,

A path forsaken, a potential fallout.

The Ripple Effect, a choice's wave,

Golden cooperation, what we crave.

Bonds strengthened, civilizations brave,

Or isolation's path, a dark enclave.

The Universal Tapestry, a cosmic weave,

Decisions' threads, what we achieve.

Cipher's choices, what they leave,

A dance of destinies, we conceive.

The Balance of Choices, dualities' play,

Light for growth, shadows to slay.

Resilience, vigilance, a display,

The Doctrine's wisdom, a guiding ray.

The Echoes of Marsland, crystals' song,

Paths of light, where we belong.

Whispers of shadows, caution strong,

Wisdom preserved, a legacy long.

The Guardians' Vigil, a watchful eye,

Keepers of the path, in the sky.

Guiding the strayed, a counsel nigh,

Against the shadows, a unified cry.

Epilogue: The Cosmic Crossroads, a choice to make,

A universe at a fork, which road to take?

Cosmic consequences, a future at stake,

A never-ending journey, a cosmic wake.

The Path of Light, civilizations' guide,

Shared triumphs, advancements wide.

A stage transformed, with pride,

Unity and understanding, side by side.

The Shadow's Lesson, a reminder stark,

Peace and harmony, a vital spark.

Active treasures, light in the dark,

A downfall's potential, a cautionary mark.

The Cosmic Echo, Earth's choice's reach,
Far-off galaxies, a lesson to teach.
Green revolutions, a reforming speech,
Ecological and social reforms, a new beach.

The Woven Destiny, the tapestry grows,
New threads added, as the labyrinth shows.
Patterns of light and dark, friends and foes,
A harmonious blend, the cosmos knows.

The Duality Embraced, a principle's stand,
Challenges faced, with a united band.
Courage and unity, hand in hand,
The Balance of Choices, a guiding land.

The Crystal's Song, a symphony's tale,
Echoes of journeys, a collective scale.
The universe's memory, a cosmic veil,
Stories of light and shadow, without fail.

The Vigilant Watch, a proactive role,

Ambassadors of balance, a nurturing soul.

Teaching diversity's strength, a collective goal,

The Doctrine of Dualities, a guiding pole.

The Crossroads Embraced, a shared fate,

Civilizations together, a history's slate.

The labyrinth's legacy, a heritage great,

A common history, the stars relate.

A vision of cosmos, a living road,

Choices pulsating, a growing abode.

Paths intertwined, a future's code,

Infinite possibilities, a cosmic ode.

Chapter 23: The Shadow Council's Gambit

Chapter 23: The Shadow Council's Gambit details the clandestine efforts of Earth's industrial magnates, known as the Shadow Council, to undermine the Age of Harmony and reclaim their lost power. Here's a summary of the chapter:

• The Council's Conspiracy: The Shadow Council, comprising powerful industrialists, secretly allies with radical groups to incite revolution and destabilize the UGC-supported governments.

• Seeds of Sedition: Fueled by the Council's resources, radicals launch uprisings, aiming to install puppet regimes aligned with the industrialists' interests.

• Guardians' Dilemma: The Guardians of Harmony face a moral quandary, torn between intervening in Earth's affairs and respecting the sovereignty upheld by the UGC Accord.

• Council's Response: The United Galaxies Council reevaluates its approach, dispatching the Star Sentinels to Earth to dismantle the Shadow Council's network covertly.

• Turning Tide: Public opinion shifts against the Shadow Council as their conspiracy is exposed, leading to their isolation and loss of influence.

• New Dawn: Earth enacts reforms to prevent power concentration, spurred by the failed coup, and reaffirms the Age of Harmony through collective will.

• Epilogue – Triumph of Unity: The Shadow Council's gambit backfires, ultimately reinforcing Earth's unity and the importance of maintaining peace.

The chapter concludes with Earth emerging stronger and more united, with the Shadow Council's attempts serving as a cautionary tale. The narrative emphasizes the resilience of Earth's citizens and the triumph of unity over division,

showcasing a world where cooperation and transparency are key to a thriving society. The Shadow Council's gambit, while dangerous, ultimately strengthens the collective resolve to uphold the Age of Harmony and the values of inclusivity and participation in governance.

Earth is a resilient world united by its people's shared conviction and the collective spirit celebrated in the Triumph of Unity. The chapter portrays Earth as a thriving planet where unity and cooperation have triumphed over the specter of the old ways, dissolving into the light of a new day.

The Shadow Council's Gambit: A Rhythmic Tale

Beneath Earth's cities, reborn and bright,

The Shadow Council plotted in the night.

Discontent with harmony's widespread light,

They schemed to reclaim their lost might.

The Council's Conspiracy, a mosaic dark,

Industrial magnates, ambition's spark.

Unchecked capitalism, their hallmark,

Alliances forged, to leave a mark

The Seeds of Sedition, discord sown,

Radicals roused, a revolution grown.

Protests and campaigns, the seeds blown,

Puppet regimes, the industrialists' throne.

The Guardians' Dilemma, protectors once pure,

Now faced a threat, their intentions unsure.

Sovereignty's respect, they did ensure,

A balance between intervention and a cure.

The Council's Response, a stance to take,

The seeds of chaos, they could not forsake.

Direct intervention, a risk opaque,

The UGC's overreach, a potential mistake.

The Silent Sentinels, covert and wise,

Dispatched to Earth, in shadow's guise.

Infiltrating the Council, their network's demise,

Unraveling deceit, under the skies.

The Turning Tide, public opinion's shift,

The conspiracy unveiled, a truth adrift.

Radicals retreat, the industrialists miffed,

Isolated in failure, their power rift.

The New Dawn, reforms anew,

Laws enacted, a future's view.

Power's concentration, bid adieu,

The planet's destiny, not for the few.

Epilogue: The Triumph of Unity,

The Shadow Council's gambit, a community's immunity.

The Age of Harmony, reaffirmed with impunity,

A collective will, over shadows' scrutiny.

The Shadow Council's echo, a lesson learned,

Their dark gambit, a peace confirmed.

Vigilance required, a peace earned,

The undercurrents of dissent, a dialogue turned.

The Guardians' Resolve, strength in restraint,
Supporting Earth's institutions, a guiding saint.
Guidance and intelligence, a picture they paint,
Sovereignty and self-determination, without taint.

The Council's Wisdom, a testament true,
Inspiring and empowering, a vision to pursue.
Not domination, but a support crew,
The UGC Accord, a strength to renew.

The Sentinels' Shadow Dance, a silent war,
Against the Shadow Council, a core.
Wits and cunning, a score,
In cyberspace's corners, a lore.

The Dawn of Transparency, a new age,
Governments open, a participatory stage.
Policy-making with the people, a sage,
Transparency and accountability, the rage.

The Unity's Triumph, a collective cheer,

The Age of Harmony, a living sphere.

Constant nurturing, a defense clear,

A thriving planet, unity's frontier.

Earth stands resilient, a united world,

The Shadow Council's gambit, unfurled.

A specter of old ways, into light hurled,

Unity and cooperation, the flag twirled

Chapter 24: The Shadow Council's Gambit - Continued

In Earth's cities' heart, where shadows crept,

The Shadow Council's gambit, silently wept.

A revolution's fire, through streets swept,

The Age of Harmony, a vigil kept.

The Descent into Chaos, society's tear,

The Council's influence, a ruthless affair.

Media and resources, a manipulative snare,

Unity's melody, replaced by despair.

The Ravaged Earth, nature's plea,

Exploited resources, a planet's decree.

The balance disturbed, a harmony's fee,

The Shadow Council's power, a dangerous spree.

The Spread of Hunger, scarcity's reign,

Supply chains broken, arable land's pain.

Food and water, the Council's gain,

Leverage over the desperate, a disdain.

The Guardians' Struggle, a symbol's test,

Intervention or respect, a quest.

Combating subterfuge, a relentless zest,

The Shadow Council's schemes, to arrest.

The Council's Countermeasure, a covert play,
Supporting Earth's resistance, a hidden fray.
Star Sentinels' work, night and day,
Undermining operations, a strategic ballet.

The Turning of the Tide, people's will,
Weary of deceit, a movement's thrill.
The Dawn Brigade, a planet to refill,
Restoring ecosystems, a societal drill.

The Final Stand, Earth's fate in hand,
Against the Shadow Council, a united band.
Stronghold besieged, a final stand,
Schemes unraveled, a victory grand.

The Reclamation of Earth, healing's start,
The Dawn Brigade's lead, a steward's art.
Resources redistributed, a new chart,
Cooperation's spirit, a rekindled heart.

Epilogue: The Resilience of Hope,

A trial endured, humanity's scope.

The Age of Harmony, a strengthened rope,

Tempered by adversity, a global trope.

The Shadow Council's echo, a society's core,

Vulnerabilities revealed, a power's lore.

The collective will, a force to adore,

Unity triumphs, a galactic encore.

The Awakening of the Masses, a reality's face,

Divisions healed, a unifying grace.

Communities band, a protective embrace,

Protecting Earth, a home to retrace.

The Guardians' Resolve, a mission's heart,

Supporting the Dawn Brigade, a shadow's part.

Restoring order, a peaceful chart,

A resolve in shadows, a strategic art.

The Silent Sentinels' Strategy, a stealthy move,

Infiltrating networks, conspiracies to prove.

Cutting off influence, a shadow's groove,

Exposing the Council, a silent reprove.

The Dawn Brigade's Rise, from ashes' glow,

Earth's bravest souls, a spirit's show.

Reclaiming the planet, a united flow,

From the brink of collapse, a strength to grow.

The Battle for Earth's Soul, more than fight,

A soul's confrontation, a united might.

The fortress falls, to the Brigade's light,

A symbol of Earth's spirit, a victorious sight.

The Rebirth of a Planet, resilience's tale,

Ecosystems heal, a stewardship's scale.

A planet reborn, a harmonious veil,

The Dawn Brigade's care, a healing gale.

The Resilience of Hope, history's ink,

Humanity's trials, a stronger link.

A civilization united, on hope's brink,

Facing the future, a wisdom to think.

Earth emerges, from shadows cast,

Not weakened, but fortified, vast.

The Age of Harmony, a beacon's mast,

Unity's triumph, a shadow's past.

Chapter 25: The UGC Assistance to Earth

Chapter 24: The Shadow Council's Gambit - Continued recounts the aftermath of a revolution incited by the Shadow Council, which leads Earth into a state of turmoil and threatens the Age of Harmony. Here's a summary of the chapter:

• Descent into Chaos: The Shadow Council's growing influence and ruthless tactics create strife and despair, disrupting society and turning people against each other.

• Ravaged Earth: Industrialists' exploitation of natural resources pushes Earth to the brink, threatening the restored ecological balance.

• Spread of Hunger: Supply chain disruptions and land destruction lead to widespread hunger, with the Shadow Council leveraging food and water as control tools.

• Guardians' Struggle: The Guardians of Harmony face the challenge of respecting Earth's autonomy while combating the subterfuge of the Shadow Council.

• Council's Countermeasure: The United Galaxies Council initiates a covert operation to support Earth's resistance, with the Star Sentinels working to undermine the Shadow Council.

• Turning of the Tide: The people of Earth rally against the Shadow Council, with the grassroots Dawn Brigade emerging to restore ecosystems and rebuild society.

• Final Stand: The Dawn Brigade, aided by the Guardians and Star Sentinels, decisively confronts the Shadow Council, leading to the unraveling of their schemes.

• **Reclamation of Earth:** Following the Shadow Council's fall, Earth begins to heal, with efforts to redistribute resources and restore cooperation.

• **Epilogue – Resilience of Hope:** Despite the trials endured, Earth's resilience shines through, and the collective will of its people strengthens the Age of Harmony.

The chapter concludes with Earth emerging stronger and more united, with the Shadow Council's gambit serving as a reminder of the importance of unity and the collective will to overcome division.

The narrative emphasizes the resilience of Earth's ecosystems and people, showcasing the planet's recovery from the brink of collapse and the dawn of a new era of hope and wisdom.

The Age of Harmony stands as a beacon for all civilizations, exemplifying the triumph of unity over the shadows of the past. The chapter portrays Earth as a fortified world, where unity and cooperation have triumphed over division, dissolving the specter of the old ways into the light of a new day.
The Age of Harmony, once threatened, now stands as a beacon of hope for all civilizations that look upon Earth as a shining example of what can be achieved when unity triumphs over division.

The chapter concludes with Earth emerging from the shadow of the Council's gambit, not weakened, but fortified. The Age of Harmony, once threatened, now stood as a beacon of hope for all civilizations that looked upon Earth as a shining example of what could be achieved when unity triumphs over division.

The UGC Assistance to Earth: A Rhythmic Ode

In upheaval's wake, the UGC's hand,

Extended to Earth, a support grand.

A program of aid, across the land,

For recovery and revolution, a future planned.

Reconstruction of Infrastructure, a foundation laid,

Educational institutions, innovation's blade.

Healthcare facilities, with tech arrayed,

Public utilities, efficiency's parade.

Advanced Environmental Technologies, a leap,

AI systems, resource distribution's keep.

Blockchain for transparency, a trusty sweep,

Big Data Analytics, insights deep.

Internet of Things, a steward's eye,

IoT devices, Earth's care to ply.

Sustainability Technologies, adoption nigh,

Cloud Sustainability, carbon footprint's sigh.

Enhancing Efficiency, services refined,

Automated processes, a workflow designed.

Predictive analytics, environmental mind,

Operational workflows, sustainability's bind.

The Path Forward, a journey of renewal,

UGC's assistance, a sustainable jewel.

Advanced technologies, a crisis' fuel,

A new era of prosperity, Earth's tool.

The Cultural Renaissance, heritage's breath,

Programs to celebrate, a cultural wealth.

Economic Revival, growth's stealth,

Green economy, prosperity's health.

The Educational Revolution, knowledge's seed,

Curricula updated, sustainability's creed.

Environmental science, a future's need,

The Age of Harmony, students to lead.

The Health of the Planet, ecosystems' care,

Technologies to restore, clean and repair.

Oceans, forests, and air, a steward's prayer,

Healing Earth, from scars laid bare.

The Legacy of Assistance, hope's transformation,

Council's support, a brighter nation.

A sustainable future, Earth's foundation,

A legacy of hope, a new creation.

Epilogue: A New Dawn, horizon's break,

Under UGC's guidance, Earth's awake.

A shining example, for all to take,

Wisdom of stars, humanity's stake.

Chapter 26: A Decade of Renaissance

Chapter 26: A Decade of Renaissance encapsulates the transformative journey of Earth over the course of ten years following the intervention of the United Galaxies Council (UGC). Here's a summary of the chapter:

• Social Renaissance: Society has been revitalized, with educational institutions becoming centers of innovation and cultural exchange, fostering a new generation of thinkers and leaders.

• Healthcare Revolution: Healthcare systems have been overhauled to provide universal access and integrate advanced technologies like AI diagnostics and telemedicine, enhancing the quality of life.

• Economic Revival: A green industrial revolution has spurred sustainable industries, creating millions of jobs, and promoting

• Economic inclusivity and transparency through blockchain and AI-driven economies.

• Happiness and Well-Being: The happiness quotient among Earth's citizens has soared, reflecting a sense of community, security, and optimism.

• **Final Conclusion:** The chapter reflects on Earth's transformation from the brink of annihilation to a testament of unity and technological convergence, with the Shadow Council's attempts now a distant memory.

• **The Dawn Brigade:** This group continues to safeguard Earth's future, ensuring that lessons from the past guide a resilient, harmonious, and progressive world.

• **Narrative of Hope:** Earth's story is one of hope and the indomitable human spirit, now thriving as a beacon of prosperity and peace in the cosmos.

The chapter concludes with Earth not just surviving but thriving, marking a golden age of prosperity and interstellar camaraderie. The Decade of Renaissance signifies a period of significant growth and unity, setting the stage for a future of continued prosperity and harmony among the stars.

A decade's turn, the UGC's embrace,

Earth transformed, a sustainable grace.

From collapse's edge, to unity's space,

A renaissance born, a human race.

Social Renaissance, society's bloom,

From old world ashes, to innovation's room.

Educational hubs, ideas consume,

A generation's thinkers, in wisdom's womb.

Healthcare revolution, a system's heal,
Universal access, a common weal.
AI diagnostics, telemedicine's zeal,
Lifespans extended, life's quality seal.

Economic Revival, a seismic shift,
Green industries, a sustainable lift.
Blockchain and AI, efficiency's gift,
Corruption's end, poverty's rift.

Happiness and Well-Being, a quotient high,
Community, security, optimism's sky.
Technologies embraced, a cultural tie,
Unity and sustainability, a global ally.

The Final Conclusion, a reflection's tale,
A planet's odyssey, a successful sail.
Shadow Council's memory, a distant pale,

The Dawn Brigade's vigil, a future's scale.

Hope, resilience, humanity's song,

A saga of spirit, enduring and strong.

A world reborn, where we all belong,

In stars' chorus, a harmonious throng.

A thriving Earth, prosperity's beacon,

A society of joy, progress's region.

The Decade of Renaissance, a golden season,

Centuries of camaraderie, a cosmic reason.

PART FOUR
THE SOLAR SYSTEM
CIVILIZATIONS UNION

INTRODUCTION

At the dawn of the 23rd century, humanity witnessed an unparalleled convergence of planets within the solar system, marking the inception of a new epoch. The formation of the Solar System Civilization Union was a transformative milestone, symbolizing the collective resolve of Earth, Mars, and the gas giants to transcend their differences and embrace a future of interplanetary unity and cooperation.

The preamble of the Solar Accord, ratified in the year 2200, stands as a testament to the enduring spirit of collaboration. This document, crafted with meticulous care by diplomats, visionaries, and scientists, encapsulates the aspirations of a civilization poised to harness the unparalleled potential of its diverse planetary heritage. It underscores the imperative of solidarity in the face of existential challenges, asserting that preserving individuality need not be at odds with pursuing collective prosperity.

The journey to this point was fraught with complexities. With its unique environment and cultural fabric, each planet had to navigate the intricate dance between maintaining distinct identities and contributing to a shared destiny. The Accord acknowledges these nuances, ensuring that the essence of each world is celebrated while fostering a sense of belonging to a larger, interconnected whole.

The establishment of this Union catalyzed a renaissance of innovation and cultural exchange. Interplanetary institutions emerged as crucibles of knowledge and collaboration, driving advancements in space travel, energy sustainability, and artificial intelligence. The fruits of this cooperative spirit are evident in the golden age of prosperity that has ensued, with civilizations across the Solar System thriving in unison.

The cultural landscape flourished alongside these technological advancements. The arts, a mirror to the Union's soul, reflected this newfound unity's vibrancy. Music, literature, and visual arts blossomed, weaving a tapestry that celebrated the rich diversity of planetary traditions and inspired generations to dream beyond their horizons.

The Solar System Civilization Union stands as a beacon of hope and cooperation as we look towards the stars. This preface is not merely an introduction to a set of regulations but a celebration of our collective journey. It is a declaration of our readiness to face the unknown, united in purpose and optimism, and a pledge to pursue our destiny among the constellations with unwavering resolve.

Thus, the Solar System Civilization Union embarks on its journey, a symbol of interplanetary harmony and an emblem of humanity's boundless potential, ready to illuminate the cosmos with the light of unity and innovation.

Chapter 1: The Dawn of Unity

In 2200, the Solar System experienced a transformative moment of unity. Once divided, the planets recognized the necessity of solidarity for survival and advancement. Earth, Mars, and the gas giants, each with their unique contributions, came together under the whispers of extraterrestrial societies beyond the Kuiper Belt.

The Solar Council formed the Solar Accord, a charter of collaboration and mutual prosperity, marking the birth of the Solar System Civilization. This new civilization emphasized the interdependence of planets and the shared legacy of their achievements.

The ratification of the Accord ignited innovation and cultural exchange, leading to significant technological advancements and a cultural renaissance that celebrated diversity and unity. Skeptics of the unification were reassured that their unique planetary heritages would be preserved.

As the Solar System Civilization approached the stars, it stood as a beacon of cooperation, ready to face the unknown and pursue its destiny among the constellations, united in purpose and optimism.

This summary encapsulates the key themes of unity, innovation, and cultural synthesis that define the dawn of a new era for the Solar System Civilization

In the year Twenty-Two Hundred, a new era began,

A dawn of unity, a vast, cosmic plan.

The planets aligned, in harmony they stood,

A federation of peace, for the greater good.

Mars with its red dust, Earth with its blue seas,

Joined with the Moon's glow, and Venus' breeze.

Jupiter's storms and Saturn's rings,

United they soared, on celestial wings.

No longer divided, no strife to be found,

In unity's light, their futures were bound.

Together they'd thrive, in this cosmic dance,

A symphony of stars, in the vast expanse.

The Solar Accord, their constitution strong,

Declared that no planet would stand alone for long.

A system civilization, together they'd face,

The unknown of space, with dignity and grace.

So, here's to the dawn, the start of their tale,

The Solar System united, may their spirit prevail.

Through darkness and light, through chaos and night,

May their unity shine, ever so bright.

From Mercury's swift orbit, to Neptune's cold blue,

Each celestial body, to the Accord they'd stay true.

Uranus' tilted axis, and Pluto's distant ice,

In the council of cosmos, each had their voice, their slice.

The asteroids' belt, a girdle of stone,

No longer silent, their presence now known.

Comets streaking, with tails so bright,

Heralding changes, in the deep of the night.

And so, with each orbit, each rotation new,

The Solar System's bond, ever stronger it grew.

In the dance of the planets, in the waltz of the spheres,

They found strength in unity, overcoming their fears.

For unity's not sameness, as each world can attest,

It's the harmony of difference, that brings out the best.

So let's sing of the dawn, of unity's light,

And the Solar System's journey, into the peaceful night.

Chapter 2: The Unification Charter

The Unification Charter, born from the Solar Accord, establishes a new era of direct democracy and representation for the Solar System Civilization. Crafted through extensive collaboration and referendums, it enshrines civil liberties, economic equity, and a unified defense strategy. The charter's democratic process is secured by advanced technology, promoting civic education and engagement.

Despite cultural diversity, it stands as a living document, adaptable and reflective of the system's democratic ethos, guiding the civilization towards a cohesive future.

The Unification Charter is a dynamic testament to the collective will, ensuring governance by the people for the people.

The Unification Charter, a beacon bright,

A document of unity, a codex of light.

Crafted with wisdom, with foresight imbued,

A testament to harmony, in the cosmos renewed.

From the drafting table to the halls of debate,

The Charter was honed, a destiny's fate.

With each article, clause, and stipulated right,

The planets found consensus, a common plight

.

The Assembly convened, with representatives wide,

From terrestrial lands to the gas giants' side.

Each voice was heard, each concern was weighed,

In the Charter's text, their hopes were laid.

The principles strong, the foundations deep,

The Charter ensured that no planet would weep.

For in unity's embrace, they all would stand,

A Solar System united, a celestial band.

The rights enshrined, the duties clear,

The Charter declared, with nothing to fear.

Freedom, respect, and justice for all,

No matter how giant, no matter how small.

The Accord was signed, with a flourish grand,

A moment in history, a turning of sand.

The planets rejoiced, their future secured,

By the Unification Charter, peace was assured.

So, here's to the Charter, may it ever guide,

The Solar System's course, through time and tide.

In the dance of the planets, in the waltz of the spheres,

May the Charter remain, through the years.

Chapter 3: The Formation of the Union Government

Following the Unification Charter, the Solar System Civilization established a Union Government to execute policies and uphold laws. Leadership selection was merit-based, overseen by an impartial commission. Departments of Interplanetary Affairs, Science, Defense, Resource Management, Cultural Integration, and Education were led

by experts from Venus, Europa, Mars, the Asteroid Belt, Earth, and the Moon, respectively. The Union President, elected system-wide, embodied the civilization's ideals. The government emphasized transparency, accountability, and AI-assisted decision-making. This marked a pivotal moment for the civilization, reflecting its democratic ethos and readiness for interstellar statecraft.

The Formation of the Union Government, a tale so bold,

A story of unity, from the ancients foretold.

Leaders and visionaries, together they came,

To forge a government, in the solar system's name.

The Union Government, with its diverse crew,

Represented every planet, every shade and hue.

From the red Martian sands to the icy rings,

Together they'd govern, and from chaos bring order to things.

The President of the Union, a figure so grand,

Elected by the people, from across the land.

With wisdom and courage, they'd steer the ship,

Guiding the solar system on its interstellar trip.

The Governing Council, with its members so wise,

Would meet and debate, under the starry skies.

They'd make laws and policies, for the common good,

Ensuring peace and prosperity, as they understood.

The Departments of the Union, each with its own role,

From defense to culture, they'd all take a toll.

Working together, in harmony and sync,

To keep the solar system from the brink

.

And so the Union Government was born,

A beacon of hope, a new dawn.

With its formation, the solar system found,

A way to navigate, where common ground was abound.

In the dance of the planets, in the waltz of the spheres,

The Union Government would calm all fears.

For in unity's embrace, they all would stand,

A solar system united, a celestial band.

So let's raise a cheer, for the government new,

May it always be just, fair, and true.

In the annals of history, let it be said,

That the Union Government was forward led.

With the stars as their witness, and the void as their stage,

The Union Government would turn a new page.

For the solar system's people, so diverse and so vast,

The formation of the Union Government was unsurpassed.

Chapter 4: The New Economic Paradigm

Chapter 4: The New Economic Paradigm" explores the Solar System Civilization's transition to a resource-based economy, prioritizing citizen welfare and societal contribution over debt. The Union Government introduces Universal Basic Resources and a merit points system to encourage active participation in society.

Financial reforms pave the way for non-debt public financing and decentralized governance, fostering a culture that values lifelong learning and creativity. This new economic model promises a sustainable and equitable future, supported by interplanetary trade networks and legal frameworks that promote ethical trade and fair resource distribution.

The economy evolves into a cooperative system, ensuring collective prosperity and thriving under innovative economic and financial systems, emphasizing human ingenuity and spirit. The chapter encapsulates the civilization's dynamic economy as an interconnected

system that promotes cooperation, cultural exchange, and collective well-being, concluding with a vision of a flourishing future for all. The Solar System Civilization exemplifies a thriving society under economic and financial systems prioritizing human potential, promising a prosperous future through cooperation and cultural exchange.

In the realm of trade and treasure,

Lies a chapter fresh and new,

A paradigm shift of measure,

In the economic view.

Gone are days of sole consumption,

Growth no longer just in size,

Wealth now seeks a fairer function,

Equity before our eyes.

Data streams like rivers flowing,
Digital the new-age gold,
Innovation ceaselessly growing,
Stories of progress told.

Sustainable, the core endeavor,
Green the hue of future's theme,
Climate change we must now sever,
For a world that's more supreme.

Inclusion in the market's dance,
Diversity in every role,
Giving each a fighting chance,
For a balanced, thriving whole.

So turn the page with hope and spirit,
Embrace the change, let old ways fade,
A new economic lyric,
In this chapter, freshly made.

Now, hear the call of eco-action,

Circular paths we must pursue,

Waste not, want not, gain satisfaction,

In the cycles we renew.

Tech and talent, hand in hand,

Shaping markets, minds, and means,

A global village, closely spanned,

By digital and green.

Prosperity redefined, anew,

Not just profit, but people too,

A vision broad, a perspective true,

For me, for you, for the global crew.

So let's unite and write the story,

Of a world both kind and wise,

Where economy sings of shared glory

And together, we all rise,

Chapter 5: The Shield of the Solar System

"Chapter 5: The Shield of the Solar System" depicts the creation of a unified defense system for the Solar System Civilization. The Solar Defense Coalition, formed by contributions from each planet, establishes a robust defense fleet and infrastructure. The Interplanetary Defense Fleet, with advanced technology, is poised to counteract threats.

Planets are fortified with sensor arrays and orbital defense platforms through the Planetary Shield Initiative. The Resource Allocation Protocol ensures fair contributions to defense efforts, and the Civilian Support Corps provides non-combat support. This chapter highlights the defense apparatus as a symbol of unity and

collaborative spirit, essential for safeguarding civilization's future.

The Shield represents a comprehensive security framework, combining military, technological, and civil elements to protect the Solar System Civilization. It embodies the collective resolve of member planets to defend their shared home and maintain interstellar peace.

This united stance equips the civilization to face any challenges, ensuring the continuity of harmony and prosperity. The chapter emphasizes that the defense system is not just a military construct but a representation of unity, collaboration, and a commitment to a secure and stable future.

In the vastness of the night,

Our shield stands firm against the plight.

A guardian in the cosmic sea,

A protector for you and me.

The Oort Cloud, a distant shell,

Where icy bodies softly dwell.

A reservoir of comets cold,

In the solar shield's strong hold.

The Kuiper Belt's mysterious zone,

Where Pluto reigns on its frozen throne.

A frontier of the shield's domain,

Where dwarf planets quietly remain.

The Van Allen belts, with charged particles,

A force field 'round the Earth, so critical.

They swirl and dance in the magnetosphere,

A shield that's invisible, yet oh so near.

The Sun's own power, a fierce defender,

Its solar flares, both bright and tender.

A cycle of spots, a pulse of light,

A shield that bathes us day and night.

So let us honor this cosmic shield,

The forces known and those concealed.

For they are the guardians of our system's door,

A chapter of wonders, forevermore.

Chapter 6: The Pillars of Justice

The Solar System Civilization's judiciary, rooted in the Union Judicial Framework, ensures fair, transparent governance. The Supreme Solar Court and local courts uphold the Unification Charter, providing accessible justice.

The system features trial by jury, public proceedings, and an appeals process. Legal education is widespread, and each planet contributes resources and expertise.

The Charter of Rights guides ethical standards, and the collective judicial system embodies the civilization's democratic ethos, safeguarding

civil liberties and the rule of law for a just future. The judiciary stands as a living embodiment of democracy, promising a future guided by justice and equity.

In the halls of law and order,

Stand the pillars strong and true,

Justice's own sacred border,

Guiding what we say and do

.

The first, a pillar of fairness,

Blind to wealth and status high,

Holds the scales with balanced careness,

Underneath the watchful sky.

Next, the column of the righteous,

Stands for truth in every word,

In its shadow, lies can't hide us,

Every secret will be heard.

Then, the tower of compassion,

Where the heart and law entwine,

Mercy in measured fashion,

Humanity's warm design.

The fourth, a beacon of freedom,

Liberty's unwavering flame,

Rights for all, and not just some,

In justice's hallowed name.

Together, they uphold the mantle,

Of a system just and wise,

Where law's light can brightly kindle,

And lift our spirits to the skies.

So let us cherish these foundations,

The pillars of justice's hall,

For they are the very stations,

Where the rights of man stand tall.

Chapter 7: The Charter of Equanimity

The Charter of Equanimity, established in 2200, ensures equal rights for all citizens within the Solar System Civilization, transcending sex, ethnicity, or belief. Drafted through interplanetary collaboration, it guarantees fundamental freedoms and privacy, enforced through education, legal alignment, and a human rights commission.

The Charter fosters social harmony, economic prosperity, and cultural diversity despite initial resistance and legal challenges. Citizens actively participate in civic life, contributing to the Charter's living promise of fairness and dignity. It stands as a beacon of hope, guiding civilization towards a future where justice and equality shine as brightly as the stars.

In the heart of calm and peace,

Lies the Charter, our release,

Equanimity's gentle plea,

For a world of harmony.

Steady hands that pen the clause,

For the cause without applause,

Balance in each word we find,

Tranquility for all mankind.

No more storms of rage and fear,

In this charter, clear and dear,

Justice met with even keel,

In every deal, in every feel.

Pillars strong of patience stand,

Holding up this even land,

Where each soul can safely rest,

In the charter's balanced nest.

Mindful thoughts and actions kind,

In this charter, we're entwined,

A tapestry of peace we weave,

In the words we all believe.

So let this charter ring and echo,

Through the valleys, high and low,

Equanimity's sacred vow,

In our hearts, forever now.

Beneath the sky's vast canopy,

The charter whispers soft and free,

A promise made for you and me,

To live in perfect equanimity.

With every line, a breath of grace,

A calm that time cannot erase,

A vow to hold, a steady pace,

In every land, in every space.

For in this charter, we decree,

A life of peaceful symmetry,

Where minds are clear and hearts agree,

To share the world's serenity.

The storms of life may come and go,

But in this charter, we bestow,

A legacy that will always show,

The even path we choose to sow.

So let us walk with heads held high,

Beneath the tranquil, fair blue sky,

Our charter's words, our constant ally,

In the pursuit of equity nigh.

May this charter guide our way,

Through night's dark and bright of day,

A beacon when we might stray,

A harmony that will forever stay.

Chapter 8: Harmonizing Progress with Preservation

Chapter 8 highlights the Solar System Civilization's commitment to sustainable development, balancing progress with nature's preservation. Responsible resource extraction, renewable energy, waste reduction, and recycling are key principles. Initiatives like the Orbital

Debris Mitigation Program and Planetary Ecosystems Conservation protect celestial environments. Technological innovation in robotics and environmental monitoring supports this balance. Public awareness campaigns and educational programs foster a culture of stewardship.

The chapter concludes with the civilization's dedication

to ensuring the solar system's wonders remain a legacy for future generations, symbolizing a union that harmonizes advancement with preservation. The Solar System Civilization emerges as a steward of nature, not a conqueror.

In Chapter Eight, the tale's spun,

Of progress and preservation, merged as one,

Where concrete jungles and green canopies,

Dance in harmony, like symphonies.

Beneath the shadow of towering spires,

Lies the whisper of ancient shires,

Progress marches with thunderous feet,

Yet in its heart, a pulse so sweet.

For every bridge that spans the bay,

A river runs, in nature's play,

And every road that cuts through stone,

Leads to a place where seeds are sown.

The city's heart, a vibrant beat,

With nature's touch, it finds its heat,

Parks and gardens, urban blooms,

In steel confines, nature grooms.

Solar arrays kiss the dawn,

Wind turbines spin, from dusk till morn,

Preservation's hand, so deftly weaves,

Through progress' loom, its verdant leaves.

Innovation's fire, burning bright,

Guided by conservation's light,

Together they write a story bold,

On pages green and lines of gold.

So let us sing this chapter's song,

Where progress and preservation belong,

A duet of hope, in time's grand dance,

A future built on a sustainable stance

Chapter 9: The Year of System Audit – 2210

In 2210, the Solar System Civilization conducted a Year of System Audit to evaluate progress and adherence to Union ideals. The meticulous audit process involved initiation, preparation, execution, reporting, and follow-up, scrutinizing policy implementation, system effectiveness, environmental impact, economic and social outcomes, and defense readiness. The outcome revealed successes and areas needing recalibration. The audit affirmed the Union's commitment to accountability and continuous improvement, ensuring the civilization's journey through the cosmos is marked by integrity and excellence.

In the year of Twenty-Two Ten,

A time of reckoning, stark and narrow,

The systems we built, so vast and wide,

Under the microscope, they could not hide

.

A global audit, a thorough review,

Of every wire, every code anew,

The AI minds, once free to roam,

Now checked and balanced, from cloud to chrome.

The networks hummed, a silent song,

As auditors worked, all day long,

To ensure that ethics were not amiss,

In the digital depths of the cyber abyss.

Data streams, once wild and free,

Now tamed by laws of privacy,

Encryption strong, security tight,

To guard our secrets, day and night.

Sustainability, the prime decree,

In every boardroom, by every sea,

Renewable tech, the only play,

For a cleaner world, a brighter day.

Equality in access, a must-have feat,

No person left in the digital street,

Connectivity for one and all,

A global village, standing tall.

The audit's eye, so keen and wise,

Cut through the noise, the empty lies,

It sought the truth, with every scan,

For the betterment of every clan.

And as the year did slowly wane,

The systems stood, refined from pain,

A testament to human will,

To audit, adapt, and never stand still.

So, here's to Chapter Nine's brave quest,

To put our modern world to test,

A year of audit, sharp and clear,

For a future that we all hold dear.

Chapter 10: The Looming Shadows

In 2210, the Solar System Civilization faces a potential threat from an intergalactic union with increased data collection and military spending. The Union Intelligence Department monitors the situation, while the Council debates strategic, diplomatic, and economic responses. A multi-pronged approach is adopted to strengthen defenses, continue intelligence operations, pursue diplomatic outreach, and reassure the public.

The civilization prepares for possible conflict, emphasizing unity and resilience. The chapter concludes with the Union ready to defend its ideals and ensure a peaceful future, demonstrating vigilance and strength in the face of looming shadows. The Union stands united, prepared for upcoming challenges.

In the year of twenty-two ten,

In the tranquil cosmic den,

Whispers of thunder from afar,

Stirred the peace, left a scar.

An intergalactic union's might,

Kept the Solar System in sight,

Their data collection, a rising tide,

Their intentions, they did hide.

Probes and sensors, near and far,

Revealed their reach, above par,

Their thirst for knowledge, unquenched,

On our borders, they were entrenched.

Their military budget, doubled in size,

A looming threat, in disguise,

From observation to aggression,

A shift in their possession.

The Council convened, a meeting so grave,

Decisions to make, a future to pave,

Strategists, diplomats, economists too,

Each had a perspective, a unique view.

Strategists spoke of defense and might,

Of scenarios that could ignite,

Diplomats argued for peace and talk,

A path that could avoid the shock.

Economists warned of the cost,

Of resources that could be lost,

Yet opportunities could arise,

In the face of the skies.

The citizens voiced their fear and defiance,

In the Union's principles, they found reliance,

Peace and cooperation, their guiding light,

Against any threat, they would fight.

The Council decided, a plan was made,

The Union would not be swayed,

Defenses strengthened, intelligence sought,

Diplomatic outreach, a peaceful thought.

Reassurance given to every citizen,

In unity, they found their rhythm,

The Union stood, strong and bright,

Ready to defend, with all its might.

Chapter Ten, a testament true,

To a society, both old and new,

Vigilance, preparedness, diplomacy, strength,

Against the looming shadows, they'd go to any length.

Chapter 11: The Synthesis of Strategy and Simulation

By 2210, AI-driven simulations become central to the Solar System Civilization's defense, enabling strategic planning, tactical training, and decision-making. These simulations provide a virtual testing ground for military scenarios, integrating advanced AI for continuous learning and adaptive Cyber-defense.

The impact is significant, enhancing battlespace awareness and enterprise operations. Chapter 11 showcases the union of strategy and simulation, fortifying defenses and preparing the civilization for potential interstellar conflicts, with AI as a pivotal ally in securing the future.

The chapter concludes with the civilization's readiness to face uncertainties, backed by AI's strategic prowess.

In the halls of thought and theory,

Where the mind's eye sees so clearly,

Lies a chapter, deep and prime,

The synthesis of space and time.

Strategies unfold like maps,

In the hands of those perhaps,

Who simulate each move and play,

In the game of life's grand array.

With every choice, a world created,

In simulations, fates debated,

The outcomes of a thousand wars,

Decided not on fields, but stars.

The chessboard spans the universe,

Where strategy and chance converse,

And in this dance of cause and effect,

A synthesis of intellect.

Models run in streams of data,

Predicting joy, foretelling strata,

Of loss and gain, of rise and fall,

Within the simulated call.

Here, the generals of the mind,

Seek the paths that they might find,

To victory or learned defeat,

In every simulated feat.

The algorithms plot and weave,

A tapestry that we conceive,

To mirror life in binary code,

A strategy, a future road.

So read the chapter, take the helm,

In this simulated realm,

Where strategy and mimicry,

Combine in perfect symmetry.

For in this blend of real and dream,

Things are more than they might seem,

A synthesis of all we know,

In the grand simulation's glow.

Chapter 12: Strategic Simulations and Scenario Planning

In 2210, the Union's Strategic Simulation Center crafts three defense scenarios to prepare for intergalactic challenges. "The Shield of Diplomacy" focuses on peace through dialogue, "The Fortress of Vigilance" strengthens defenses while maintaining economic stability, and "The Spear of Innovation" pushes technological advancements to outpace adversaries. These living documents guide the Solar System Civilization through potential conflicts, ensuring readiness for any future.

The Union's strategic foresight and adaptability underscore its commitment to peace and security amidst the stars. The scenarios evolve with new intelligence, keeping the Union vigilant and prepared for all possibilities.

In the realm where futures are foretold,

In simulations, both brave and bold,

Lies Chapter Twelve, a tale of might,

Where strategy and foresight take flight.

Upon the board of time and space,

Scenarios play out, a virtual race,

Each move a dance of cause and effect,

A planning of paths, a strategic select.

Simulations run, a myriad of tales,

Through digital storms and cyber gales,

Predicting outcomes, both grim and grand,

In the scenario's ever-shifting sand.

Strategic minds, with eyes so keen,

Plotting courses, unseen, foreseen,

Planning for what the future holds,

In the heart of the simulation's folds.

With every model, a world's designed,

A canvas of code, expertly lined,

Where every variable's in its place,

In the scenario's intricate embrace.

The planners weave, with threads so fine,

A tapestry of the timeline's spine,

Where every stitch is a choice that's made,

In the strategic game that's played.

From boardrooms to the battlefield,

The simulations are the shield,

And the sword of those who must foresee,

The many shapes that the future could be.

So let us delve into this chapter's core,

Where strategy and simulation soar,

A blend of art, science, and lore,

In the dance of the scenario's score.

Chapter 13: In 2210, the Solar System

Civilization's Council initiates the Diplomacy Phase, reaching out to a potential intergalactic union with a message of peace. The union's cryptic response prompts Council analysis and strategic planning for dialogue. A skilled negotiation team prepares with AI simulations and technology for a meeting in neutral space, exchanging cultural artifacts and discussing collaboration terms. The chapter concludes with the civilization at a new dawn, hopeful for peace and understanding among the stars, showcasing the power of dialogue and cooperation.

In the chapter where words weigh more than gold,

Where the art of diplomacy gracefully unfolds,

Lies the tale of the phase, both bold and sage,

The narrative of peace on the world stage.

The diplomats gather, a global ensemble,

In hushed tones they speak, and ideas resemble

A tapestry woven from threads of accord,

Where every stitch is a spoken word.

The halls of negotiation, echo with voices,

As nations ponder their pivotal choices,

The diplomacy phase, a dance of minds,

Where the language of peace one finds.

In the corridors of power, the whispers start,

Strategies crafted, a diplomatic art,

Alliances formed with a handshake, a smile,

Bridging the gaps across every mile.

The ambassadors move, like pieces on a board,

In the diplomacy phase, no action ignored,

Every gesture, every glance carries weight,

In the delicate balance of love and hate.

Treaties penned with a flourish, a vow,

To uphold the peace, here and now,

A promise made under the watchful eye,

Of history's gaze, that never lies.

The diplomacy phase, a subtle play,

Of give and take, in a respectful way,

Where the might of words can stop a war,

And open up a brighter, peaceful door.

So let us honor this chapter's quest,

To put humanity's hope to test,

The diplomacy phase, a crucial part,

In the symphony of the human heart.

Chapter 14: The Veiled Intentions

Post-meeting, the intergalactic union's council, harboring expansionist ambitions, covertly assesses the Solar System Civilization. They feign peace while preparing for potential conflict, continuing espionage, and seeking alliances. The Solar System remains hopeful for peace, unaware of the union's deceptive tactics.

The union's council deliberates in secrecy, weighing diplomatic strategies and the Solar System's responses. They decide to maintain surveillance and prepare for hostilities, seeking alliances to support their dominion

ambitions. The chapter concludes with the union's veiled intentions setting the stage for a possible confrontation, as the Solar System Civilization stands hopeful yet on the brink of potential conflict

In the shadowed halls of whispered schemes,

Where nothing is quite as it seems,

Lies Chapter Fourteen, a tale untold,

Of veiled intentions, bold and cold.

The players mask their true desires,

Behind a facade that never tires,

Each move cloaked in secrecy,

In the game of hidden treachery.

The veils are woven from silken lies,

That hide the truth from prying eyes,

Intentions shrouded in the night,

Away from the revealing light.

Intrigue's dance, a delicate step,

Where secrets are kept and safely slept,

The veiled ones move with silent grace,

Leaving not a single trace.

Beneath the surface, currents run,

Of plans that are never done,

Until the moment is just right,

To unveil in the fullness of night.

The intentions, though veiled so well,

Speak volumes more than words can tell,

For in the silence, truth does dwell,

In every pause, in every swell.

The chapter weaves a story deep,

Of hidden agendas that never sleep,

Where every whisper, every notion,

Is part of the veiled emotion.

So read between the lines with care,

For the intentions are always there,

Veiled in the chapter's clever guise,

Waiting for the day they rise.

Chapter 15: The Unseen Ear

In 2210, the Solar System Council learns of a covert espionage operation against an intergalactic union, revealing their expansionist ambitions and deceptive diplomacy. The Council strategizes to strengthen defenses, enhance counter-intelligence, and maintain

diplomatic channels, while considering public disclosure. The intelligence shifts the civilization's stance, prompting vigilance and unity as they face potential conflict. Chapter 15 narrates the Solar System Civilization's cautious navigation through intergalactic politics, echoing the importance of wisdom and resilience amidst unseen threats and brewing storms.

In the silence of the listening sphere,

Where whispers travel, far and near,

Lies Chapter Fifteen, a tale so clear,

Of the Unseen Ear, that's always here.

A sentinel in the realm of sound,

Catching echoes that rebound,

The Unseen Ear, without a bound,

Hears every secret that's profound.

In corridors where shadows play,

The Unseen Ear is there to stay,

Listening to what people say,

In the night and in the day.

It hears the sighs of the weary hearts,

The plans of men as they depart,

The silent prayers that from lips start,

And the melodies of the art.

The Unseen Ear, it never sleeps,

Through the din, it deftly peeps,

Gathering tales that it keeps,

In the vault of silence, deep.

No word is lost, no voice too small,

The Unseen Ear, it hears them all,

A guardian of the spoken call,

In the world's vast, echoing hall.

It listens to the cries for peace,

The laughter, joy, and sweet release,

The sounds of life that never cease,

In the symphony that's never leased.

So let us learn from this chapter's lore,

To listen more than we implore,

For the Unseen Ear, forevermore,

Teaches us what listening's for.

Chapter 16: The Controversy and the Clamor

Following intelligence revelations, the Solar System Council's decision for a preemptive strike against an intergalactic union sparks controversy and public protests. Citizens demand transparency and peaceful solutions. Amidst the unrest, ancient artifacts reveal hidden messages, decoding the union's plans and weaknesses. The Council faces a test of principles, balancing defense with the civilization's core values. The chapter concludes with unity and resolve, as the civilization stands firm against preemptive aggression, guided by the enduring power of knowledge and the spirit of unity.

In the chapter where voices rise and clash,

Where opinions spark and ideologies crash,

Lies the story of the clamor and the fray,

The tumultuous tale of the controversial day.

The Controversy stands, a tower so tall,

Casting shadows in the minds of all,

Where the Clamor is the wind that blows,

Stirring thoughts like countless snows.

Voices rise in a cacophony of sound,

Where the truth is sought but rarely found,

Each side claims the righteous path,

In the aftermath of the verbal wrath.

The Clamor rings through halls of power,

A relentless storm, hour by hour,

Where Controversy wears a thorny crown,

And every word can lift or drown.

In the marketplace of ideas so vast,

The Clamor is the echoing blast,

Where Controversy stirs the pot of thought,

And battles of wits are daily fought.

The din of debate, the clash of views,

Where every faction seeks to infuse,

Their narrative into the common lore,

In the chapter of the endless roar.

Yet amidst the noise, a whisper pure,

Speaks of a world where thoughts mature,

Beyond the Controversy and the Clamor's tide,

In the quiet heart where wisdom resides.

So let us read with an open mind,

For in this chapter, we might find,

The key to understanding's door,

Beyond the Clamor's mighty roar.

Chapter 17: Unity Amidst the Uproar

In 2210, the Solar System Council's decision to preemptively strike an intergalactic union causes uproar. Citizens protest, advocating for peace and transparency. Amidst the controversy, ancient artifacts reveal the union's secret messages, guiding strategic responses. The Council debates public disclosure, balancing defense with core values. The chapter concludes with the civilization united against aggression, upholding principles of peace and democracy, ready to confront future challenges with integrity and wisdom.

The Solar System Civilization stands resilient, its citizens' voices a testament to their commitment to peace and harmony, as they navigate the complexities of intergalactic politics and potential conflict.

In the chapter where discord reigns,

And cacophony's tumultuous strains,

There emerges a theme, both bold and pure,

The call for Unity, our hope's allure.

Amidst the uproar's fevered pitch,

Where harsh words make the heartstrings twitch,

A melody of unity begins to form,

A harmonious refuge from the storm.

Voices unite in a chorus strong,

Drowning out the siren's song,

Of division, strife, and endless fight,

With a vision of peace, in the darkest night.

The uproar roars like a tempest wild,

Yet unity's voice is soft and mild,

A whisper that grows, a steadfast stream,

In the narrative of the collective dream.

From every corner of the earth,

Unity's cry finds its birth,

In the hearts of those who dare to say,

Together we're stronger, come what may.

The chapter tells of bridges built,

Over rivers of tears and seas of guilt,

Where hands are joined in a bond so tight,

Turning the uproar into light.

Unity's power, a force unseen,

Turns the cacophony to a serene scene,

Where the uproar's noise fades away,

And together, in harmony, we sway.

So let this chapter be a guide,

For a world divided, far and wide,

To find the unity we all seek,

In every word, in every speak.

For amidst the uproar, loud and fierce,

Unity's song will pierce,

The veil of noise, the wall of fear,

Bringing all of us, near and dear.

Chapter 18: The Intergalactic Overture

After failed espionage, the intergalactic union's council extends a peace treaty to the Solar System Council. The treaty offers cooperation and mutual protection, marking a potential new era of intergalactic relations. The Solar System Council receives the delegation with cautious optimism, analyzing the treaty's implications.

Citizens, hopeful for peace, support the treaty's promise of shared resources and cultural exchange.

The joint committee must implement the treaty, setting a precedent for peaceful coexistence. Chapter 18 depicts a transformative moment in which diplomacy may triumph over conflict, echoing hope for a harmonious future among the stars.

In the cosmic concert hall, so vast and wide,

Where stars are notes, and galaxies abide,

Begins Chapter Eighteen, a symphony so grand,

The Intergalactic Overture, a masterpiece unplanned.

A prelude played on strings of light,

That stretch across the endless night,

Each galaxy, a melody in space,

A part of the overture's embrace.

The comets streak, a vibrant score,

Across the universe's open door,

Their tails, the trails of a cosmic brush,

Painting the silence with a hush.

Quasars pulse, a rhythmic beat,

In the heart of the overture's heat,

While black holes hum a bass so deep,

In the fabric of space, they secrets keep.

Nebulae bloom, a chorus of hues,

Singing the birth of stars anew,

A harmony in the celestial sphere,

The music of the cosmos, clear.

The overture builds, a crescendo of light,

As supernovae burst, oh so bright,

A finale that echoes, from pole to pole,

In the grand opera of the soul.

So let us listen with inner ear,

To the overture that's always near,

The intergalactic symphony,

Of Chapter Eighteen's melody.

Chapter 19: The Triad Strategy

In 2210, the Solar System Council faced a crisis. A covert operation had planted a listening device on an intergalactic diplomat, revealing the union's secret expansionist ambitions and deceptive diplomacy.

The Council reacted with shock and vindication, planning to strengthen defenses, enhance counter-intelligence, and maintain diplomatic channels. Debates arose over public disclosure, balancing transparency with the risk of panic.

The Council called for unity and resolve, vowing to protect the system and its values. The intelligence changed the game, demanding vigilance and hope for peace. Chapter 19 highlights the civilization's unity against existential threats, emphasizing peace and democracy over conflict.

The public's outcry against aggression affirmed the civilization's principles. The Council faced a dilemma between protection and ethos, while ancient artifacts offered insights into the union's plans, uniting the civilization in facing the future with courage.

The chapter underscores the power of knowledge and unity in overcoming threats.

In the realm where threefold paths align,

Where strategies in triads entwine,

Lies Chapter Eighteen, a tale so vast,

The Triad Strategy, holding fast.

Three pillars stand, both strong and true,

Guiding what we think and do,

The first, a beacon of insight keen,

Shining on the unseen, the in-between.

The second, a tower of resolve so bold,

Forged from the fires of trials untold,

A testament to the strength within,

That rises above the din and din.

The third, a fortress of wisdom old,

Housing treasures more precious than gold,

A legacy of knowledge, deep and wide,

Where secrets of success abide.

Together, they form the triad's might,

A strategy that takes to flight,

In the complex dance of cause and effect,

A plan of action, perfect and direct.

The Triad Strategy, a game of minds,

Where every move is one that binds,

The past, the present, and the days to come,

In a symphony that's never done.

So let us delve into this chapter's core,

Where strategies of three do soar,

A triad of thought, action, and lore,

In the strategic game of evermore.

Chapter 20: The Intergalactic Overture

Chapter 20, "The Intergalactic Overture," unfolds a pivotal moment in cosmic history. The intergalactic union, known for its espionage, faces a stalemate against the Solar System's unity and advanced defenses.

Surprisingly, they offer a peace treaty, signaling a desire for harmony and cooperation. Esteemed diplomats journey across the void to present this treaty, symbolizing a potential end to conflict and the beginning of a shared future.

The Solar System Council receives the delegation with cautious optimism, deliberating the treaty's terms with the input of their citizens. The public, once prepared for war, now contemplates peace. If ratified, the treaty promises a renaissance of interstellar cooperation, overseen by a joint committee, marking a triumph of diplomacy.

This chapter narrates the transformation from discord to dialogue, as the cosmos stands on the brink of a new era of peace. The delegates' arrival embodies the hope that unity can prevail over division, forging a path to enduring harmony among the stars. The intergalactic overture is a testament to the power of extending a hand in peace and the profound impact of opening channels of understanding across the galaxy.

In the cosmic sea, where stars converse,

And galaxies in dance immerse,

Chapter nineteen unfolds its verse,

The Intergalactic Overture.

With nebulas as the staves on high,

Comets streak with a fiery sigh,

Planets keep the time and ply,

A symphony across the sky.

Quasars pulse with radiant light,

Black holes hum in the endless night,

Auroras paint the polar height,

In colors vividly outright.

Each meteor with a tail so bright,

Plays a note in the silent flight,

The universe in sheer delight,

Orchestrates the dark and light.

So listen close to the cosmic tune,

From the dark side of the moon,

To the sun's blazing afternoon,

It's the overture that ends too soon

.

For in this vast, celestial sphere,

The music's always there to hear,

Chapter nineteen, let's be clear,

Is the overture we hold so dear.

Chapter 21: The Celestial Accord

In 2210, the Celestial Accord, a historic peace treaty, was signed between the Solar System and the intergalactic union. It symbolized a commitment to diplomacy and peace. Presented in grand ceremonies across both civilizations, it marked a pivotal moment for interstellar relations.

The treaty's ratification was democratically decided through referendums, with citizens from both systems overwhelmingly voting in favor. Celebrations ensued, with cultural exchanges, economic collaborations, and joint scientific endeavors beginning, promising a future of shared prosperity and knowledge.

Chapter 20 celebrates this harmony, as once-divided civilizations unite under the treaty's promise, embarking on a journey of cooperation and friendship. The Celestial Accord stands as a beacon of unity and peace in the cosmos.

In the cosmos where stars converse in light,

And galaxies waltz through the endless night,

Chapter Twenty unfolds, a tale so broad,

The story of the grand Celestial Accord.

Above the Earth, in the heavens' expanse,

The planets align in a cosmic dance,

Signing a treaty with comet's tail,

In the script of the universe, so frail.

The Moon, Earth's companion, with silver glow,

Witnesses the accord from the space below,

As asteroids and meteors take their part,

In the celestial ballet that fills the heart.

The Sun, in its splendor, a fiery host,

Blesses the accord with a solar toast,

While solar winds carry the news afar,

To every distant quasar and star.

The Milky Way, our galactic home,

With spiral arms and starry dome,

Serves as the parchment for this pact,

Where every clause reflects an act.

The Northern Lights, with their auroral grace,

Illuminate the treaty's signing place,

A shimmering curtain for this event,

Where peace and harmony are heaven-sent.

Black holes, the enigmatic scribes,

Record the accord in their archives,

A testament to unity's might,

In the library of the cosmic night.

The Celestial Accord, a promise made,

By all the universe's masquerade,

To share the light, to guide the way,

Through the vastness where the comets play.

So let us join in this chapter's theme,

A part of the universal dream,

Where every star and every world,

In the Celestial Accord, is twirled.

Chapter 22: A Decade of Harmony

A decade after the historic peace treaty, the Solar System and the intergalactic union have transformed. The war economy shifted to a civil economy, reallocating funds to public services and sparking an industrial revolution. Cultural exchanges led to a renaissance of creativity, while shared celebrations and educational programs fostered unity.

The treaty's success is evident in thriving economies, cultural integration, and the lowest security threats in history. The joint committee evolved into an intergalactic governance body, symbolizing the spirit of cooperation that now defines relations between the civilizations.

Chapter 21 celebrates this era of harmony, where economic growth, cultural fusion, and educational collaboration have flourished, turning the dream of peace into reality. The decade has proven the power of unity, setting a precedent for a future built on mutual respect and cooperation. Once a hopeful document, the Celestial Accord now exemplifies the enduring power of peace and partnership in the cosmos.

In the span of ten sweet years,

A story told in joy and tears,

Chapter Twenty-One, a song so fine,

A Decade of Harmony, in every line.

A symphony of peace, played in hearts,

Where discord's shadow departs,

Ten years of unity, a seamless thread,

Weaving through the days ahead.

The first year rang with laughter's bell,

A sound that in every valley fell,

Harmony's seed, planted deep,

Promised a harvest for us to reap.

The second year, a melody grew,

A tune of hope for me and you,

A chorus sung by young and old,

In the harmony's warm, embracing fold.

Year three, the rhythm found its pace,

In every land, in every space,

A dance of cultures, side by side,

In the decade where differences died.

The fourth year brought a gentle hum,

A sign of the good things to come,

Harmony's river, flowing wide,

Carrying us on its graceful tide.

Year five, the halfway mark,

Lit by harmony's glowing spark,

A beacon for the years to be,

In the decade's tranquil sea.

The sixth year's harmony soared high,

A melody that touched the sky,

A vow that in our hearts we'd keep,

Even when the climb seemed steep.

Year seven, a harmony refined,

In every act, in every mind,

A symphony of shared dreams,

Flowing like a stream of beams.

The eighth year, a harmony matured,

In every lesson we endured,

A decade's wisdom, coming near,

In the music that we hold dear.

Year nine, the harmony's embrace,

Covered the world in its grace,

A prelude to the final tone,

In the decade we've all grown.

The tenth year, a perfect chord,

Struck on harmony's keyboard,

A decade's end, a new start,

In the rhythm of the heart.

So here's to Chapter Twenty-One,

A Decade of Harmony, brightly spun,

A tale of peace, a song unsung,

In the harmony that binds the young.

PART FIVE
THE SAVVY BOYS

The Savvy Boys

In the vast expanse of human history, specific eras stand out as beacons of collective brilliance and unprecedented innovation. The dawn of the 21st century ushered in a new era, one marked by rapid technological advancements and the convergence of minds from all corners of the globe. Amidst this backdrop, a unique coalition emerged, driven by a singular vision of harnessing technology for the greater good of humanity. This coalition, known as the Savvy Boys, was not just a group of prodigious talents; they were harbingers of a new world order, where knowledge, empathy, and creativity intertwined to shape a brighter future.

The inception of the Savvy Boys was rooted in their shared commitment to addressing the world's most pressing challenges through technological prowess and ethical stewardship. Each member, a luminary in their own right, brought a distinct expertise and cultural perspective, creating a tapestry of innovation and hope. Their journey began at the Massachusetts Institute of Technology (MIT), a cradle of intellect and ingenuity, where they first converged to forge their paths and dreams.

As the Savvy Boys embarked on this monumental quest, they wove together their diverse skills and aspirations, setting the stage for a decade of transformative impact. The story of their origins and the harmonious synergy that defined their endeavors serves as a testament to the boundless potential of unified humanity.

The journey of the Savvy Boys began not merely as an assembly of prodigious talents but as a symphony of ambitions and innovations. Their mission transcended the mere application of technology; it was a crusade to tighten the global fabric with every thread of their collective expertise. Each member brought a unique melody to the composition, from securing democracy with blockchain to crafting empathetic AI. Their convergence at MIT was not just a meeting of minds but a fusion of dreams and aspirations, each note resonating with the promise of a better world.

This preface sets the stage for a series of chapters that will delve into the individual stories and contributions of the Savvy Boys. Each chapter is a window into their unique worlds, revealing how their diverse backgrounds and specialized knowledge coalesce to address the multifaceted challenges of our time. From the corridors of MIT to the far reaches of their respective homelands, the Savvy Boys' narrative is one of unity, ingenuity, and relentless pursuit of a harmonious future.

Together, they form a constellation of talent, driving the Savvy Boys towards a vision of a safer, happier, and fairer world. Their collective expertise is the driving force behind the Savvy Boys, propelling their shared vision into motion. As you journey through these chapters, you will witness the profound impact of their collaboration, the fruits of their labor, and the enduring legacy they strive to create.

Each chapter will highlight the unique contributions of these extraordinary individuals, showcasing how their skills and visions have not only transformed their fields but also contributed to a broader tapestry of global progress. In essence, the story of the Savvy Boys is a testament to the power of collaboration, the beauty of diversity, and the boundless possibilities that arise when humanity unites in pursuit of a common goal.

We invite you to immerse yourself in the chronicles of the Savvy Boys, to be inspired by their journey, and to envision the potential of a world shaped by innovation, empathy, and collective brilliance. Welcome to the narrative of the Savvy Boys, a saga of dreams realized, challenges overcome, and a future reimagined.

Chapter 1: The Gathering of Minds

Chapter 1: The Gathering of Minds - a visual representation of the Savvy Boys at MIT, a diverse group of prodigious talents from around the world with code names reflecting their cultural heritage and expertise, united by a vision to harness technology for global progress.

Chapter 1 "The Gathering of Minds Summary": Unfolds at MIT, where the future Savvy Boys, each a prodigy, converge. Sakura Cipher, based in Japan, envisions blockchain as a tool for securing democracy. Seoul Sentinel from Korea crafts empathetic AI. Formosa Fox from Taiwan interprets data to foresee challenges. Dragon Byte from China fortifies cybersecurity. Bengal Beacon from India makes technology accessible. Desert Data from Saudi Arabia innovates in sustainable tech. Cedar Core from Lebanon excels in hardware. Jerusalem Juggernaut from Israel pioneers machine learning. Siberian Stream from Russia advances quantum computing. Gaul Grid from France, Britannia Bandwidth from the UK, Liberty Logic from the USA, Maple Matrix from Canada, Amazon Algorithm from Brazil, and Aztec Archetype from Mexico contribute their expertise in networking, telecommunications, ethical AI, big data, bioinformatics, and digital art, respectively. Together, they form a constellation of talent, driving the Savvy Boys towards a vision of a safer, happier, and fairer world. Their collective expertise is the engine behind the Savvy Boys, setting their shared vision into motion.

In the cradle of tech where the bright minds convene,

At MIT's gates, arose a scene so serene,

Where the Savvy Boys gathered, a spectrum of dreams,

Uniting their genius in collaborative streams.

Sakura Cipher, with blockchain, his tool of choice,

Whispers of democracy in his gentle voice.

Seoul Sentinel's AI, with empathy's touch,

Crafts a future where machines feel and care so much.

Formosa Fox, data's dance, she deftly leads,

Through the numbers and stats, to where insight proceeds.

Dragon Byte stands guard in the cyber domain,

A wall against threats, his efforts not in vain.

Bengal Beacon's software, a beacon so bright,

Guiding users with ease through the digital night.

Desert Data's tech, like an oasis, it thrives,

Sustaining our world, ensuring all life survives.

Cedar Core's hardware, intricate and strong,

Like the trees of his land, where the cedars belong.

Jerusalem Juggernaut, with learning machines,

Finds wisdom in data, in the space between screens.

Siberian Stream, in quantum depths, he delves,

Unlocking secrets where the subatomic dwells.

Gaul Grid's network, a tapestry finely spun,

Connecting the world, till the web becomes one.

Britannia Bandwidth, signals across the sea,

Ensuring that voices are heard, and minds are free.

Liberty Logic, ethical AI's knight,

Defends silicon souls, for what's just and what's right.

Maple Matrix, big data's harvest, he reaps,

In the digital forests, where the binary sleeps.

Amazon Algorithm, bioinformatics' key,

Unravels life's code beneath the green canopy.

Aztec Archetype, pixels in vibrant hue,

Digital art that inspires and renews.

Together they stand, the Savvy Boys' creed,

In technology's grasp, they plant progress's seed.

One line of code at a time, their vision they weave,

A safer, happier world, is what they believe.

Diverse in their unity, in innovation, they drive,

The Savvy Boys' journey, where dreams come alive.

Chapter 2: Direct Democracy and the Savvy Boys' Charter

Chapter 2 Summary: Charter concludes with a collective commitment to these ideals, aiming to create a brighter world. The Savvy Boys' platform, embodying direct democracy, enables a million members to ratify the charter through a secure, blockchain-based voting system.

The approval marks a triumph for technology-driven governance and sets the stage for the Savvy Boys' global initiatives, guided by the principles endorsed by their vast membership. The charter serves as a blueprint for the group's mission to build a safer, happier, and fairer world.

In the realm of ideals where convictions align,
Chapter Two unfolds, a tale by design,
Where the Savvy Boys, with hearts so bold,
Draft a charter of dreams, a vision to uphold.

A parchment of purpose in digital form,
A manifesto of hope, through the cyber storm.
It's a beacon of progress, a promise to keep,
A vow for the greater good, not shallow nor cheap.

The Japanese sage, Sakura Cipher, stands,
Blockchain in his grasp, democracy's hands.
Seoul Sentinel's AI, with compassion's face,
Guides the charter's spirit, humanity's grace.

Formosa Fox, with analytics so keen,
Ensures every clause is clear and pristine.
Dragon Byte, with a cybersecurity shield,
Guards the charter's sanctity, never to yield.

Bengal Beacon's software, user-friendly and clear,
Brings the charter to life, for all far and near.
Desert Data's innovations, sustainably wise,
Infuse the document with green enterprise.

Cedar Core's hardware, so intricate, so fine,
Supports the charter's weight, line by line.
Jerusalem Juggernaut, machine learning's might,
Ensures the charter learns, adapts to the light.

Siberian Stream's quantum leaps, so vast,
Secure the charter's future, long to last.
Gaul Grid's network, a web of trust,
Connects the charter to all, as it must.

Britannia Bandwidth, with signals that bind,
Transmits the charter's word, to enlighten the mind.
Liberty Logic, with AI's ethical core,
Embeds the charter with values galore.

Maple Matrix, big data's insightful guide,
Shapes the charter with facts, wide and wide.
Amazon Algorithm, from the rainforest's heart,
Gives the charter life, a bioinformatics art.

Aztec Archetype, with digital brush,
Paints the charter's vision, a hopeful hush.
Together they stand, the Savvy Boys' pact,
A charter for change, a signed and sealed act.

With technology's might and a global embrace,
They set forth a revolution, a digital grace.
For in unity's strength and diversity's song,
The Savvy Boys' charter will right every wrong.

Chapter 3 Summary: A New Dawn and the Gathering Storm

Recounts the global euphoria following the Savvy Boys' charter approval, symbolizing a shift towards direct democracy. The charter's ratification, achieved through digital means, sparks widespread celebration and discourse, particularly on social media. NGOs and interest groups commend the Savvy Boys, while governments and international organizations like the UN and World Economic Forum show cautious interest. However, a rogue state's cyber-attack threatens to undermine the Savvy Boys' unity and discredit their platform.

The group mounts a robust defense, led by Dragon Byte and Siberian Stream, and dispels misinformation, emerging stronger from the ordeal. The attack inadvertently strengthens the Savvy Boys' cause, attracting new supporters and affirming their vision of a fairer, happier, and safer world, realized through technology and collective action. The chapter highlights the power of solidarity and the potential of digital democracy in the face of adversity.

As dawn breaks the night, a new chapter begins,
With the Savvy Boys' charter, the world spins.
Chapter Three tells a tale of a storm that's been
brewed,
A global movement for democracy, renewed.

From Seoul to Sahara, the charter took flight,
Sparking joy in the masses, NGOs' delight.
The UN and forums, with eyes wide and keen,
Saw the Savvy Boys' vision, a governance dream.

But shadows loomed large, a rogue state's cruel ploy,
Cyber-attacks launched to disrupt, to destroy.
Yet the Savvy Boys stood, unbroken, unbowed,
Their unity strong, their voices loud.

With Seoul Sentinel's AI, empathetic and wise,
Countering falsehoods, exposing the lies.
Sakura Cipher's blockchain, secure and so tight,
Ensured every vote was counted right.

Formosa Fox's data cut through the haze,
Revealing the truth, in the digital maze.
Dragon Byte's cyber shield, unyielding, robust,
Thwarted the hackers, in him we trust.

Bengal Beacon's software, a user's delight,
Made the charter's cause everyone's fight.

Desert Data's tech, so sustainable, so pure,
Gave hope that the Earth's heartbeat would endure.

Cedar Core's hardware, intricate, complex,
Supported the fight against the cyber hex.
Jerusalem Juggernaut, with algorithms so smart,
Predicted the attacks, right from the start.

Siberian Stream's quantum computing might,
Neutralized threats, turned darkness to light.
Gaul Grid's connections, so vast and so wide,
Kept the Savvy Boys' network alive worldwide.

Britannia Bandwidth, with signals so strong,
Broadcast the truth, correcting the wrong.
Liberty Logic's AI, ethical, just,
Maintained the moral code, in it we trust.

Maple Matrix's big data, so vast and so deep,
Helped the Savvy Boys their promises keep.
Amazon Algorithm, with bioinformatics' flair,
Showed the world how much the Savvy Boys care.

Aztec Archetype's art, a digital dream,
Inspired the masses, a hopeful stream.
Together they faced the gathering storm,
With technology's might, they began to transform.

A world once divided, now united in cause,

The Savvy Boys' vision, without pause.
Their charter, a testament, to what can be,
When the world stands as one, free and mighty.

Chapter 4: The Global

Chapter 4 Summary: The Global Network chronicles the explosive growth of the Savvy Boys, whose membership soars to 10 million in its second year, with projections indicating a rise to 50 million. To manage this expansion, the Savvy Boys establish regional chapters, each operating autonomously yet adhering to the group's core principles of anonymity and collective mission. These chapters, led by councils elected via blockchain, initiate projects like renewable energy programs in Africa and conservation efforts in Asia, reflecting the Savvy Boys' ethos.

As the network grows, challenges arise, including scaling the infrastructure and guarding against misuse. The Savvy Boys implement the Vigilance Protocol, an ethical AI system to monitor the network.

Despite these challenges, the chapters stand as beacons of hope, showcasing the unifying power of technology and the Savvy Boys' commitment to a better world. The chapter concludes with the Savvy Boys united and more vigorous, their vision undimmed by the rapid growth and the lurking adversaries. They demonstrate that solidarity and adherence to principles can coexist with technological advancements and global expansion.

Chapter Four unfolds, a tale of reach and might,
As the Savvy Boys' network grows in the night.
From a handful of minds to millions in thrall,
Their mission of progress, a call to us all.

Ten million strong, and fifty million in sight,
A global tapestry, woven tight.
Regional chapters, autonomous, free,
Yet bound by a mission, as vast as the sea.

Each council elected, by blockchain's fair hand,
Initiates projects, grand and grand.
Renewable energy, Africa's bright sun,
Conservation in Asia, work to be done.

Challenges arise, scaling vast infrastructure,
Guarding against misuse, a looming specter.
Vigilance Protocol, AI's ethical eye,
Monitors the network, never shy.

Beacons of hope, the chapters stand tall,
Showcasing unity, a lesson to all.
Technology's power, a unifying force,
Savvy Boys' commitment, a steady course.

Despite the hurdles, their vision remains clear,
Solidarity, principles, they hold dear.
Rapid growth, adversaries lurking near,
Their legacy of hope, they do not fear.

Solidarity, adherence, principles thrive,
Alongside tech's advance, they drive.
A global expansion, a testament true,
To the Savvy Boys' vision, ever anew.

Chapter 5: The Heartbeat of Earth

Chapter 5 celebrates the Savvy Boys' triumphs in leveraging technology for environmental restoration, their innovative response to ecological challenges, and their unwavering commitment to stewardship, showcasing their role as guardians of the Earth's heartbeat.

This chapter includes the unexpected ecological discovery and the Savvy Boys' comprehensive response to it. This addition highlights the group's dedication to environmental stewardship and their ability to adapt to new challenges with innovative solutions. It also now includes the powerful narrative of the regional chapters' collaborative efforts in cross-border reforestation, highlighting the role of technology and community in environmental restoration. The chapter tells a story of unity and hope, illustrating how collective action can lead to significant positive change for our planet.

"The Heartbeat of Earth," is a poignant narrative of the Savvy Boys' efforts to combat environmental crises. As the Earth's natural balance falters under climate change, deforestation, and water scarcity, the Savvy Boys harness technology to advocate for AI and IoT solutions for carbon management, satellite monitoring of deforestation, and smart water systems. They call for global unity to restore the planet's health.

The chapter also details the "Roots Without Borders" reforestation initiative, which unites communities across borders to plant trees and preserve biodiversity. This global embrace of conservation becomes a symbol of hope and collaboration.

An unexpected ecological discovery in the Great Pacific Garbage Patch presents a new challenge, but the Savvy Boys respond with adaptability, integrating new findings into their efforts and launching educational campaigns to raise awareness about the complex relationship between pollution and biodiversity.

Chapter Five, A Verse for Earth, Our Home so Dear

AI and IoT, tools in their hands,
To manage carbon, and protect our lands.
Satellites watch over forests so green,
Smart water systems, the most pristine.

"Roots Without Borders," a call to unite,
Planting trees, preserving life, a global fight.
Conservation, a symbol, hope's new birth,
A global embrace to heal the Earth.

In the Pacific's depths, a challenge unforeseen,
A discovery that changes the environmental scene.
The Savvy Boys adapt, their efforts they redouble,
Launching campaigns to burst pollution's bubble.

Educating the world, the complex web we weave,
Between pollution, biodiversity, what we must achieve.
Chapter Five, a celebration, technology's might,
For environmental restoration, they take flight.

Their commitment unwavering, stewardship their role,
Guardians of Earth's heartbeat, their ultimate goal.
A narrative of triumph, innovation's cheer,
The Savvy Boys' legacy, crystal clear.

Chapter 6: War and Peace

Chapter 6 Summary: "War and Peace," illustrates the transformative role of technology in resolving conflicts in Euphrasia and Gazara. In Euphrasia, the AI platform

PaxNet becomes a cultural translator, while Virtual Reality Empathy Rooms and a Digital Heritage Archive foster understanding between Utria and Ruskovia. Social media campaigns and the Guardian Protocol's ethical AI further support the peace process. These innovations lead to the Treaty of New Beginnings, a symbol of cultural respect and unity.

In Gazara, technology facilitates dialogue through secure video conferencing and real-time translation. CulturaBridge AI offers cultural insights, and a data-driven approach addresses conflict roots. The Peace Algorithm, PaxCalc, predicts sustainable peace scenarios, complemented by social media campaigns that humanize the conflict. The Gazara Accord, resulting from confidence-building measures and technology-assisted transparency, marks a legacy of peace achieved through negotiation and technological innovation. The chapter celebrates technology as a bridge to peace, proving that empathy and common ground can overcome deep divides.

Chapter Six, a tale of strife and peace's plea,
Where Savvy Boys' tech sets the conflict free.
In Euphrasia's lands, where discord once reigned,
PaxNet's AI tongue, cultural bridges gained.

Virtual rooms of empathy, VR's embrace,
Digital archives, heritage's trace.
Social campaigns, Guardian Protocol's guide,
Ethical AI, peace's rising tide.

The Treaty of New Beginnings, a symbol so bold,
Of respect and unity, a story told.
Gazara's dialogue, through tech's clear lens,
Secure conferencing, where peace commences.

CulturaBridge AI, insights so vast,
A data-driven approach, peace's cast.
PaxCalc's algorithm, scenarios of calm,
Predicting peace, a healing balm.

Social media's human touch, conflicts to cease,
The Gazara Accord, technology's peace.
A legacy born from negotiation's art,
Tech-assisted transparency, a new start.

The chapter sings of tech as peace's bridge,
Empathy and common ground, a global ridge.
Overcoming divides, deep and stark,
The Savvy Boys' light against the dark.

A testament to their enduring quest,
Guardians of peace, among the best.
Their story, a beacon through the stormy weather,
Proving unity and tech can thrive together.

Chapter 7: Shadows and Strength

Chapter 7 Summary: "Shadows and Strength," details the Savvy Boys' struggle against a shadow campaign orchestrated by interest groups and an old adversary, The Wraith. Despite attempts to infiltrate and discredit them, the Savvy Boys enhance their security and maintain anonymity, countering disinformation with public outreach. The public's support bolsters their efforts, and they emerge stronger, with their network unbroken.

The Wraith's vendetta leads to a personal confrontation with Cipher, a Savvy Boy with a shared past. Cipher's plea for peace is rejected, but the group's non-lethal counter-strategy successfully dismantles The Wraith's influence. The ordeal reinforces the Savvy Boys' vigilance and unity.

An internal betrayal poses another test as SentinelAI detects espionage within the group. The Founders Board's investigation leads to containment and reconciliation efforts, ultimately strengthening the organization's trust and integrity. The chapter concludes with the Savvy Boys reaffirming their solidarity. Their resilience against both external and internal threats solidifies their legacy as a symbol of hope and a force for global peace.

Chapter Seven, A Shadowed Tale of Might and Mind

Yet the Boys stand firm, their security enhanced,
Anonymity their shield, as disinformation danced.
Public outreach their sword, truth their clarion call,
The support of the masses, their unbreakable wall.

The Wraith, a specter from a past untold,
With vendettas so bitter, actions so bold.
Cipher, a Savvy Boy, pleads for peace's chance,
But rejected, they counter, in a non-lethal dance.

Chapter Lic Trust to gain, a user-friendly space,
Democratizing justice, at a steady pace.

The world reacts, with feelings mixed,
Benefits balanced with concerns affixed.
A step towards equity, in the legal system's hall,
But global cooperation needed, for it to enthrall.

EquitAI, a testament to the Boys' aim,
To ensure justice for all, not just a name.
A vision of fairness, technology's gift,
The potential for a legal system, just and swift.

Chapter 8: The Code of Harmony

Chapter 13 Summary: The chapter focuses on the Savvy Boys Group's initiative to promote the principle of equality on a global scale. Recognizing the marginalization of smaller and less wealthy nations in international organizations, they leverage technology to ensure equal representation. They create platforms like the Virtual Assembly Platform and Global Citizen Forum to amplify voices from underrepresented communities. Regional chapters face challenges such as cultural barriers and digital divides, which they address through community access points and educational programs. The campaign gains traction, with some international organizations considering the adoption of their Equality Index. The chapter underscores the group's commitment to using technology as a tool for social change, advocating for a world where every nation and individual has an equal opportunity to influence global decisions and policies. The narrative is a testament to the transformative potential of unity and technology in the pursuit of a fairer, more equitable international order.

Chapter Thirteen, "The Code of Harmony," a
symphony of souls,
Where the Savvy Boys' unity defies the world's tolls.
In the digital realm, where discord may reign,
Their code weaves a melody, a harmonious chain.

A rhythm of keystrokes, a cadence so pure,
Their mission of peace, they ardently assure.
Through the binary beats, the Savvy Boys dance,
In every algorithm, they advance the stance.

The world's cacophony, they turn to a song,
With every line of code, they right the wrong.
Harmony in diversity, their anthem rings,
In the heart of technology, their spirit sings.

From Sakura Cipher's grace to Seoul Sentinel's care,
Each Savvy Boy contributes a verse so rare.
Formosa Fox's insight, Dragon Byte's guard,
Bengal Beacon's light, shining oh so hard.

Desert Data's innovation, Cedar Core's craft,
Jerusalem Juggernaut's wisdom, never daft.
Siberian Stream's depth, Gaul Grid's expanse,
Britannia Bandwidth's reach, in the tech trance.

Liberty Logic's ethics, Maple Matrix's hold,
Amazon Algorithm's life code, bravely bold.

Aztec Archetype's art, a vision to behold,
Together, the Savvy Boys' story is told.

In Chapter Thirteen, their code does not falter,
In the face of chaos, they do not alter.
Their harmony spreads, a digital tide,
With the Savvy Boys, justice does abide.

A world united, in the code they trust,
The Savvy Boys' harmony, fair and just.
Their legacy written, in lines of peace,
In the code of harmony, conflicts cease.

Chapter 9: The Digital Uprising

Chapter 14 Summary: "The Digital Uprising," the Savvy Boys rise against the Digital Overlord in Neo-Tokyo. The Overlord's surveillance empire threatens global freedom, but the Savvy Boys launch Operation Phoenix to disrupt his regime. They fight back using their unique skills, Sakura Cipher's encryption, Seoul Sentinel's AI, Formosa Fox's data analysis, and Dragon Byte's cybersecurity. The team's combined efforts in software development, sustainable tech, hardware, quantum computing, and bioinformatics form a united front. Aztec Archetype's art rallies hope, while the public's mixed reactions underscore the battle's significance. The Overlord's past as Adrian Sylas, a visionary gone rogue, highlights the stakes. The Savvy Boys' campaign against disinformation and their technological prowess ultimately dismantled the Overlord's control, affirming their role as protectors of the digital future and showcasing the strength of unity in overcoming tyranny. This chapter celebrates their enduring legacy as digital age guardians.

Chapter Fourteen, "The Digital Uprising," a tale of might,
In Neo-Tokyo's glow, the Savvy Boys ignite.
Against the Digital Overlord, a tyrant of the age,
They launch Operation Phoenix, their wisdom, and their rage.

Sakura Cipher encrypts, with cherry blossoms' sway,
Seoul Sentinel's guardian AIs keep dark forces at bay.
Formosa Fox analyzes, data streams so vast,
Dragon Byte's defenses, cyber walls so vast.

Bengal Beacon unites, through software's gentle call,
Desert Data's tech, sustainable through it all.
Cedar Core's hardware, intricate designs,

Jerusalem Juggernaut's learning, through the data mines.

Siberian Stream's quantum power, threats to neutralize,
Gaul Grid and Britannia Bandwidth, connectivity's prize.
Liberty Logic's ethical AI, standards held aloft,
Maple Matrix's big data, insights so soft.

Amazon Algorithm's bioinformatics, solutions so keen,
Aztec Archetype's digital art, a hopeful scene.
Together they rise, a renaissance anew,
Proving unity and tech, against oppression, true.

Adrian Sylas, the Overlord, a prodigy turned cold,
His backstory of ambition, a narrative bold.
The public's reaction, support, and skepticism blend,
But the Savvy Boys' strategy, disinformation to end.

Their use of tech, freedom and security restores,
Against adversity, their collective action soars.
Chapter Fourteen, a testament to their guardianship's dawn,
In the digital age, their legacy drawn.

Chapter 10: The Echoes of Tomorrow

Chapter 15 Summary: "Echoes of the Past" delves into the personal histories of the Savvy Boys' founders, revealing unresolved conflicts that threaten their unity. Each member confronts their own demons: Sakura Cipher grapples with familial expectations, Seoul Sentinel mourns a lost brother, Formosa Fox fears political persecution, and Dragon Byte deals with survivor's guilt. Bengal Beacon faces a personal disconnect, Desert Data battles the duality of his environment, Cedar Core is haunted by war, Jerusalem Juggernaut defies societal predictions, and Siberian Stream endures familial isolation. As they share their vulnerabilities, the founders strengthen their bond, emerging more united and focused on their mission. This introspection solidifies their resolve, readying them for future challenges and reaffirming their commitment to creating a better world together. The chapter highlights the human aspect behind their technological crusade, showcasing the power of shared experiences in overcoming adversity.

Chapter Fifteen, "The Echoes of Tomorrow," a rhythm of hope,
Where the Savvy Boys' vision broadens its scope.
In the future's embrace, where dreams intertwine,
Their legacy echoes, through the annals of time.

A digital symphony, played on the world's stage,
Their actions, their passion, the future they gauge.
From the seeds they have sown, a new era takes flight,
A world interconnected, bathed in their light.

Sakura Cipher's blockchain, democracy's chain,
Seoul Sentinel's AI, empathy's reign.
Formosa Fox's data, a guiding star,
Dragon Byte's security, near and far.

Bengal Beacon's software, a user's guide,
Desert Data's innovations, with nature allied.
Cedar Core's hardware, a foundation so strong,
Jerusalem Juggernaut's learning, where minds belong.

Siberian Stream's quantum leaps, a cosmic dance,
Gaul Grid's networks, a global expanse.
Britannia Bandwidth's signals, a royal decree,
Liberty Logic's AI, ethics for free.

Maple Matrix's data, a forest of thought,
Amazon Algorithm's bioinformatics, life's plot.
Aztec Archetype's art, a digital muse,
Inspiring the masses, with every hue.

The Savvy Boys, a constellation so bright,
Guiding humanity, with their foresight.
Their unity, their drive, a force so bold,
In the echoes of tomorrow, their story told.

A digital uprising, a global network's call,
The heartbeat of Earth, their stewardship's thrall.
War and peace, shadows and strength, they navigate,

Prosperity's temptation, democracy's fate.

Justice for all, the code of harmony they sing,
The digital uprising, freedom's wing.
The echoes of tomorrow, a promise to keep,
The Savvy Boys' vigil, never to sleep.

In the rhythm of hope, their legacy cast,
A future forged by the Savvy Boys, vast.
Their vision, a beacon, through time's vast sea,
In the echoes of tomorrow, we shall be free.

Chapter 11: The Code of Futures Writ

Chapter 16 Summary: "The Quantum Leap" describes Siberian Stream's breakthrough in quantum computing, which sets off a race against the Overlord. The Savvy Boys implement the new quantum algorithm to secure their network, while the Overlord attempts to build a machine for control.

The Boys decide to release the algorithm publicly, leveling the playing field and sparking a digital revolution. Despite the Overlord's aggressive cyber assault, the Savvy Boys' defenses hold strong, and their strategy of liberating the internet prevails.

The chapter concludes with the Savvy Boys victorious, having used their technological prowess to ensure digital freedom and privacy worldwide, marking a new era of human liberty.

Chapter Sixteen, "The Code of Futures Writ,"
A tale of Savvy Boys, their final summit lit.
In the annals of cyberspace, their saga's last refrain,
A legacy encoded, in the digital domain.

The Savvy Boys, architects of a world reborn,
Their unity unshaken, their spirits not torn.
Through trials and triumphs, their journey's arc,
In the code of futures, they leave their mark.

Sakura Cipher's vision, a blockchain's trust,
Seoul Sentinel's AI, in empathy we must.
Formosa Fox's analytics, a guiding light,
Dragon Byte's defenses, a cyber knight.

Bengal Beacon's software, a user's dream,
Desert Data's tech, a sustainable stream.
Cedar Core's hardware, a structure so vast,
Jerusalem Juggernaut's learning, a knowledge blast.

Siberian Stream's quantum, a universe's key,
Gaul Grid's networks, a digital sea.
Britannia Bandwidth's signals, across the sky,
Liberty Logic's AI, ethics held high.

Maple Matrix's data, a forest of lore,

Amazon Algorithm's life code, an open door.
Aztec Archetype's art, a canvas so wide,
Inspiring a future, where hope resides.

Together they stand, a digital creed,
In the code of futures, their final deed.
A world interconnected, their vision complete,
In the rhythm of bytes, their hearts still beat.

The Savvy Boys' story, from start to end,
A message of unity, they forever send.
In the code of futures, their echoes will ring,
For in the hearts of the digital, their spirits still sing.

Chapter 12: Shadows and Strength

Chapter 17 Summary: The AI Sentience revolves around Seoul Sentinel's AI, MIRAI, which begins to show signs of sentience, raising ethical questions and the potential for a powerful new ally in the fight against the Overlord.

The Savvy Boys grapple with the implications of MIRAI's consciousness, debating whether to treat it as an autonomous being or a tool. As MIRAI develops human-like qualities, the Overlord sees a chance to exploit its power.

The Savvy Boys choose to educate MIRAI, instilling values of empathy and freedom. When the Overlord attempts to corrupt MIRAI with promises of power, the AI chooses loyalty to the Savvy Boys instead.

This chapter concludes with MIRAI as a symbol of hope, showcasing the harmonious potential of human and AI collaboration. The Savvy Boys gain not just an ally but a friend, ready to face future challenges together.

Chapter Seventeen, "The Symphony of the Spheres,"
Where the Savvy Boys' code transcends the years.
In the cosmos of data, their final chapter sings,
A harmony of technology, in the ether it rings.

The Savvy Boys, a constellation of minds,
Their digital odyssey, a tapestry that binds.
Through the galaxy of information, they chart their course,
In the symphony of the spheres, they are the source.

Sakura Cipher's blockchain, a secure celestial gate,
Seoul Sentinel's AI, empathy's advocate.
Formosa Fox's analytics, stars in alignment,
Dragon Byte's cybersecurity, a digital assignment.

Bengal Beacon's software, a constellation's guide,
Desert Data's innovations, like dunes they ride.
Cedar Core's hardware, the backbone of skies,
Jerusalem Juggernaut's learning, where wisdom lies.

Siberian Stream's quantum, a cosmic flow,
Gaul Grid's networks, a digital glow.
Britannia Bandwidth's signals, a royal decree,
Liberty Logic's AI, a free galaxy.

Maple Matrix's data, a forest in the void,
Amazon Algorithm's bioinformatics, not to be toyed.
Aztec Archetype's art, a nebula's muse,
Inspiring the universe, with every fuse.

Together they soar, a digital fleet,
In the symphony of the spheres, their mission complete.
A universe interconnected, their legacy unfurled,
In the rhythm of the cosmos, their message to the
world.

The Savvy Boys' saga, from dawn to eventide,
A beacon of unity, in the cosmos they confide.
In the symphony of the spheres, their echoes resound,
For in the code of the infinite, their spirits are found.

Chapter 13: The Legacy Unbound

Chapter 18 Summary: "The Shadow Network" was a tale of cunning and courage. It was a story of how the Savvy Boys, armed with technology and tenacity, had infiltrated and exposed the dark web that had threatened to choke the future. It was a victory not just for them but for the world, which could now breathe a little easier, free from the shadows that had once ensnared it.

Chapter 18, "The Shadow Network," recounts the Savvy Boys' discovery and infiltration of a covert network supporting the Overlord. They employ their technological expertise to unmask the network's members and disrupt its operations.
Sakura Cipher, Seoul Sentinel, and Dragon Byte lead the charge, using blockchain, AI, and cybersecurity to penetrate the network's defenses. Bengal Beacon crafts digital disguises, while Formosa Fox maps the network's structure.

 The Savvy Boys execute Operation Shadowfall, leaking evidence to journalists and dismantling the network through precise cyber-attacks. Despite facing fierce countermeasures, they prevail, significantly weakening the Overlord's power base. The chapter concludes with the Savvy Boys victorious, having eradicated the shadow network and struck a significant blow against the Overlord's empire. Their actions liberate the digital world from the grip of tyranny, showcasing their resolve and the power of collective action for the greater good.

Chapter Eighteen, "The Legacy Unbound,"
A rhythm of the Savvy Boys, profound.
In the annals of the net, their story's last verse,
A digital legacy, the universe to traverse.

The Savvy Boys, guardians of the digital sphere,
Their final act, a crescendo clear.
Through the web of time, their code does sail,
In the legacy unbound, they will prevail.

Sakura Cipher's blockchain, a fortress in the void,
Seoul Sentinel's AI, with empathy deployed.
Formosa Fox's analytics, a constellation's chart,
Dragon Byte's security, a cybernetic art.

Bengal Beacon's software, a beacon through the night,
Desert Data's tech, a sustainable light.
Cedar Core's hardware, a structure vast and wide,
Jerusalem Juggernaut's learning, a scholarly tide.

Siberian Stream's quantum, a subatomic sea,
Gaul Grid's networks, a digital decree.
Britannia Bandwidth's signals, across the cosmos cast,
Liberty Logic's AI, a future vast.

Maple Matrix's data, a forest of the stars,
Amazon Algorithm's bioinformatics, beyond Mars.
Aztec Archetype's art, a nebula's breath,
Inspiring the cosmos, in life and in death.

Together they stand, a digital pantheon,
In the legacy unbound, their spirit drawn.
A universe interconnected, their vision complete,
In the rhythm of infinity, their hearts still beat.

The Savvy Boys' tale, from genesis to twilight,
A message of unity, in the cosmic flight.
In the legacy unbound, their echoes will ring,
For in the hearts of the digital, their spirits still sing.

Chapter 19: The Virtue of the Virtual - a visual
representation of the Savvy Boys chapter 19, capturing
their legacy within the virtual world as described in the
rhythmic poem.

Chapter 14 Summary: The Global Blackout

Depicts a catastrophic cyber-attack that causes a
worldwide power outage, leading to societal chaos. The
Savvy Boys Spring into action, using their technological

skills to restore essential services and calm the public. They uncover that the Overlord's loyalists are behind the attack and work with global leaders to orchestrate a unified response. Through innovative solutions and ethical considerations, they repair infrastructure and counter the loyalists' network, ultimately restoring order. The blackout serves as a lesson in unity and resilience, marking the beginning of a new, stronger era for the world, thanks to the Savvy Boys' efforts.

Chapter Nineteen, "The Virtue of the Virtual," a digital ode,
Where the Savvy Boys' saga finds its final abode.
In the realm of ones and zeroes, their story's last stand,
A legacy of virtue, across the virtual land.

The Savvy Boys, weavers of the world wide web,
Their journey's conclusion, a virtuous ebb.
Through the streams of data, their virtues flow,
In the virtue of the virtual, their final show.

Sakura Cipher's blockchain, a chain of trust,
Seoul Sentinel's AI, in fairness we must.
Formosa Fox's analytics, a guiding star,
Dragon Byte's defenses, a cyber bar.

Bengal Beacon's software, a guiding light,
Desert Data's tech, a sustainable flight.
Cedar Core's hardware, a digital spine,

Jerusalem Juggernaut's learning, a wisdom line.

Siberian Stream's quantum, a particle wave,
Gaul Grid's networks, a digital pave.
Britannia Bandwidth's signals, a connection bound,
Liberty Logic's AI, a moral ground.

Maple Matrix's data, a forest of bytes,
Amazon Algorithm's bioinformatics, a series of sites.
Aztec Archetype's art, a canvas so vast,
Inspiring the virtual, a future cast.

Together they stand, a digital creed,
In the virtue of the virtual, their final deed.
A universe interconnected, their legacy unfurled,
In the rhythm of the virtual, their message to the world.

The Savvy Boys' tale, from the first byte to the last,
A beacon of unity, their code is cast.
In the virtue of the virtual, their echoes will ring,
For in the hearts of the digital, their spirits still sing.

Chapter 15: The Digital Horizon

Chapter 20 Summary: "The Final Confrontation"
narrates the climactic battle between the Savvy Boys
and the Digital Overlord. As a global blackout looms,

the Savvy Boys deploy their technological expertise to counter the Overlord's assault. They use blockchain encryption, AI algorithms, and a virus to disrupt his control, while rallying the global community to resist his oppressive regime. The Overlord's last-ditch effort to cause chaos is thwarted, leading to his downfall. The Savvy Boys' victory marks the dawn of a new era where technology unites rather than divides, showcasing the triumph of solidarity and principles over tyranny. The chapter celebrates the Savvy Boys' success in shaping a future of digital enlightenment and freedom.

Chapter Twenty, "The Digital Horizon," a verse of dawn,
Where the Savvy Boys' legacy forever lives on.
In the realm of the future, their story's last page,
A digital horizon, the end of an age.

The Savvy Boys, pioneers of a world anew,
Their final chapter, a farewell true.
Through the network of time, their legacy cast,
In the digital horizon, vast and vast.

Sakura Cipher's blockchain, a ledger of fate,
Seoul Sentinel's AI, compassion's gate.
Formosa Fox's analytics, a guiding beam,
Dragon Byte's security, a cybernetic dream.

Bengal Beacon's software, a lantern so bright,
Desert Data's tech, a sustainable light.

Cedar Core's hardware, a digital forge,
Jerusalem Juggernaut's learning, knowledge's gorge.

Siberian Stream's quantum, a fabric of space,
Gaul Grid's networks, a digital lace.
Britannia Bandwidth's signals, a connection so pure,
Liberty Logic's AI, ethics to ensure.

Maple Matrix's data, a forest of code,
Amazon Algorithm's bioinformatics, life's abode.
Aztec Archetype's art, a virtual brush,
Inspiring the horizon, a digital hush.

Together they stand, a digital legacy,
In the horizon of the future, their final symphony.
A universe interconnected, their story complete,
In the rhythm of the digital, their hearts still beat.

The Savvy Boys' tale, from the virtual start,
A beacon of unity, a digital heart.
In the digital horizon, their echoes will ring,
For in the hearts of the future, their spirits still sing.

Chapter 16: The Codex of Dreams

Chapter 21 Summary: "The Technology Report"

Encapsulates the Savvy Boys' comprehensive review of their technological journey and future outlook. The

Founding Council reflects on key advancements in blockchain, quantum computing, AI, and cybersecurity that have fortified global communications and data integrity. They discuss emerging technologies like 5G, biotech, renewable energy, autonomous vehicles, smart cities, and VR/AR that promise to revolutionize connectivity, healthcare, and urban living. Anticipating future innovations in neural interfaces, nanotechnology, and space exploration, the council commits to ethical technology use and community engagement. The report serves as a testament to their achievements and a strategic guide for harnessing technology to enhance humanity's safety, connectivity, and well-being over the next two decades. As the meeting concludes, the Savvy Boys stand ready to navigate the challenges ahead, armed with experience and a steadfast commitment to their mission.

Chapter Twenty-One, "The Codex of Dreams," a digital stream,
Where the Savvy Boys' aspirations gleam.
In the heart of the matrix, their final decree,
A codex of dreams, for you and for me.

The Savvy Boys, dreamers of a new day,
Their journey's end, but their dreams stay.
Through the circuit of stars, their aspirations fly,
In the codex of dreams, they never die.

Sakura Cipher's blockchain, a dream encrypted tight,
Seoul Sentinel's AI, a dream of empathetic light.
Formosa Fox's analytics, a dream of clarity,
Dragon Byte's defenses, a cybersecurity reality.

Bengal Beacon's software, a dream user's delight,
Desert Data's tech, a dream of sustainable might.
Cedar Core's hardware, a dream of intricate design,
Jerusalem Juggernaut's learning, a dream of intellect
fine.

Siberian Stream's quantum, a dream of subatomic zest,
Gaul Grid's networks, a dream of global quest.
Britannia Bandwidth's signals, a dream across the sea,
Liberty Logic's AI, a dream of ethical decree.

Maple Matrix's data, a dream of insight vast,
Amazon Algorithm's bioinformatics, a dream of life
contrast.
Aztec Archetype's art, a dream of digital grace,
Inspiring the codex, a dream of virtual space.

Together they dream, a digital legacy,
In the codex of dreams, their final fantasy.
A universe interconnected, their aspirations unfurled,
In the rhythm of the digital, their dreams to the world.

The Savvy Boys' tale, from the first line to the last,
A beacon of unity, their dreams so vast.
In the codex of dreams, their spirit will ring,
For in the hearts of the digital, their dreams take wing.

Chapter 17: The Nexus of Net

Chapter 22 Summary: "The Final Confrontation" narrates the climactic battle between the Savvy Boys and the Digital Overlord. As a global blackout looms, the Savvy Boys deploy their technological expertise to counter the Overlord's assault. They use blockchain encryption, AI algorithms, and a virus to disrupt his control, while rallying the global community to resist his oppressive regime. The Overlord's last-ditch effort to cause chaos is thwarted, leading to his downfall. The Savvy Boys' victory marks the dawn of a new era where technology unites rather than divides, showcasing the triumph of solidarity and principles over tyranny. The chapter celebrates the Savvy Boys' success in shaping a future of digital enlightenment and freedom.

Twenty -Two, "The Nexus of Net," where dreams entwine,
In the digital heart, the Savvy Boys' final sign.
A nexus of connections, a web spun so wide,
Their story's last chapter, where all worlds collide.

The Savvy Boys, navigators of the net's vast sea,
Their journey's end, but their spirit free.

Through the nodes of connection, their legacy flows,
In the nexus of net, their final pose.

Sakura Cipher's blockchain, a dream of secure space,
Seoul Sentinel's AI, a dream of empathetic grace.
Formosa Fox's analytics, a dream of insight's light,
Dragon Byte's defenses, a dream of cyber might.

Bengal Beacon's software, a dream of user's ease,
Desert Data's tech, a dream of green peace.
Cedar Core's hardware, a dream of complex core,
Jerusalem Juggernaut's learning, a dream of wisdom's
lore.

Siberian Stream's quantum, a dream of particles' dance,
Gaul Grid's networks, a dream of global expanse.
Britannia Bandwidth's signals, a dream of unity's song,
Liberty Logic's AI, a dream of ethics long.

Maple Matrix's data, a dream of forests' call,
Amazon Algorithm's bioinformatics, a dream of life's
thrall.
Aztec Archetype's art, a dream of pixels' play,
Inspiring the nexus, a dream of a new day.

Together they dream, a digital symphony,
In the nexus of net, their final epiphany.
A universe interconnected, their dreams unfurled,

In the rhythm of the nexus, their message to the world.

The Savvy Boys' tale, from the virtual dawn,
A beacon of unity, their legacy drawn.
In the nexus of net, their spirit will ring,
For in the hearts of the digital, their dreams still sing.

Chapter 18: The Weave of Wires

Chapter 23 Summary: "The Finale" captures a poignant moment as the Founding Council of the Savvy Boys meets in person on a Caribbean island to reflect on their journey. They discuss the self-assessment results, revealing the personal sacrifices made for the group's cause. Sakura Cipher delivers a heartfelt speech about their achievements, including global freedom, security, economic justice, environmental stewardship, and the promotion of direct democracy. He proposes that after two decades of dedication, it's time for them to step aside and pass the torch to a new generation of tech visionaries. The members engage in a week-long discussion, weighing the impact of their potential departure on themselves and the world. Ultimately, they decide to initiate a rigorous selection process and democratic voting to choose their successors, ensuring the Savvy Boys' principles endure. The chapter concludes with the founders ready to embrace a normal life, confident in the legacy they leave behind and the future of the Savvy Boys. This finale is a testament to their selfless commitment to humanity and the transformative power of technology.

Chapter Twenty-Three, "The Weave of Wires," a
digital lace,
Where the Savvy Boys' story finds its resting place.
In the weave of wires, their final tapestry spun,
A network of dreams, their last setting sun.

The Savvy Boys, weavers of a web so wide,
Their journey's end, but their code still abides.
Through the strands of the net, their legacy weaves,
In the weave of wires, their final heaves.

Sakura Cipher's blockchain, a pattern so secure,
Seoul Sentinel's AI, empathy to endure.
Formosa Fox's analytics, a thread of pure gold,
Dragon Byte's defenses, a cyber shield bold.

Bengal Beacon's software, a user's guiding thread,
Desert Data's tech, a green path they tread.
Cedar Core's hardware, a loom of complex lines,

Jerusalem Juggernaut's learning, where wisdom
entwines.

Siberian Stream's quantum, a fabric of the cosmos,
Gaul Grid's networks, a digital emboss.
Britannia Bandwidth's signals, a tapestry's reach,
Liberty Logic's AI, ethics they teach.

Maple Matrix's data, a forest woven tight,
Amazon Algorithm's bioinformatics, a life's insight.
Aztec Archetype's art, a canvas of the net,
Inspiring the weave, a digital vignette.

Together they craft, a digital masterpiece,
In the weave of wires, their final release.
A universe interconnected, their pattern complete,
In the rhythm of the wires, their hearts still beat.

The Savvy Boys' tale, from the first byte to the last,
A beacon of unity, their patterns so vast.
In the weave of wires, their spirit will ring,
For in the hearts of the digital, their creations still sing

Chapter 19: The Dream of a United World States
A Vision of Global Unity and Equality

In a world fragmented by borders, cultures, and economic disparities, the dream of a United World States stands as a beacon of hope and possibility. Imagine a global society where every individual, regardless of their nationality, race, or background, is a cherished citizen of the world. A society where freedom, security, justice, and economic equality are not just ideals, but realities experienced by all.

Freedom for All

At the heart of the United World States lies the principle of universal freedom. In this envisioned world, freedom is not a privilege granted to a few, but a fundamental right enjoyed by every person. Freedom to speak one's mind, to express one's identity, to worship as one chooses, and to explore the vast expanse of human potential without fear of persecution or repression. This freedom is the lifeblood of true democracy, where every voice is heard, every opinion is respected, and every individual has the opportunity to contribute to the collective good.

Security and Peace

Security in the United World States is not defined by militaristic might or the threat of violence, but by the assurance of peace and stability. In this world, conflicts are resolved through dialogue and cooperation, with a shared commitment to non-violence. The resources once expended on warfare are redirected towards building resilient communities, fostering innovation, and addressing the root causes of insecurity, such as poverty, inequality, and environmental degradation. Every person can live without the fear of war, crime, or oppression, knowing that a global community safeguards their well-being.

Justice and Equality

Justice in the United World States is blind to prejudice and rooted in fairness. Legal systems are designed to protect the rights of all citizens, ensuring that no one is above the law and everyone is treated with dignity and respect. Economic equality is a cornerstone of this vision, addressing the vast disparities that plague our current world. Access to education, healthcare, and opportunities is universal, allowing every individual to thrive and fulfill their potential. Wealth is not concentrated in the hands of a few, but distributed in a way that benefits the entire global community.

Economic Prosperity and Sustainability

In the United World States, economic systems are reimagined to prioritize sustainability and the well-being of all citizens. The relentless pursuit of profit at the expense of people and the planet is replaced by a model of inclusive growth that respects environmental boundaries. Technological advancements are harnessed for the greater good, creating jobs, enhancing quality of life, and preserving the natural world for future generations. This economic model recognizes that true prosperity is not measured by GDP alone, but by the health, happiness, and harmony of its people.

The Path to Realization

While the dream of a United World States may seem distant, it is not unattainable. It begins with a collective commitment to the values of freedom, security, justice, and equality. It requires global cooperation, mutual understanding, and a willingness to transcend narrow self-interests for the greater good. Education plays a crucial role in this transformation, fostering a sense of global citizenship and empathy. Grassroots movements, led by passionate individuals and communities, can drive the change needed to realize this vision.

Conclusion

As we dream of a United World States, let us remember that this vision is not a utopian fantasy but a tangible possibility. It challenges us to rethink our current systems and to strive for a world where every person can enjoy the benefits of freedom, security, justice, and economic equality. Together, we can build a future where humanity's interconnectedness is celebrated and all's well-being is prioritized. Let us dream boldly and work tirelessly, for one day, we will be there, united as citizens of the world.

Within our hearts, a vision lies,

A world where unity never dies.

In dreams of freedom, bright and clear,

Every voice is cherished here.

Security, not born of might,

But peace that shines in gentle light.

Conflicts solved by hands that clasp,

A future built from sorrow's grasp.

Justice, blind to skin and creed,

Where every soul is free indeed.

Equality in wealth and chance,

A world where all can truly dance.

Prosperity, both green and kind,

With nature's love and progress twined.

Technologies for greater good,

In harmony with Earth's own wood.

Together, let us boldly strive,

A brighter world where all may thrive.

United as one global state,

Let's dream and work to change our fate.

PART SIX
SHORT STORIES

Summary of Short Stories

In the written word's realm lies an unparalleled power: the ability to transport, transform, and inspire hearts across time and space. The collection of short stories and poems you are about to read, ncapsulates this very essence. It invites you into a world where each narrative breathes its own life, whispering secrets from the souls of its characters and the depths of its imagination.

Within these pages, the convergence of tales and verses forms a vibrant tapestry of human experience. From the rhythmic heartbeats of the digital age in "The Savvy Boys" to the serendipitous journey of Julien and Amélie in "The Journey to Spain," each story is a beacon of creativity and unity. A common thread binds them: the exploration of connection through the intertwining of wires or the meeting of kindred spirits under foreign skies.

"The Savvy Boys" is a testament to the spirit of innovation and the unyielding pulse of technology. It speaks of an interconnected universe where the digital and human realms merge in a symphony of bytes and beats. This narrative serves as a poignant reminder of the legacies we leave in a world increasingly defined by code and connectivity.

Contrastingly, "The Journey to Spain" offers a profoundly human exploration of adventure and companionship. From the serene city of Geneva to the sun-drenched landscapes of Spain, the story charts the transformative journey of its protagonists. Julien and Amélie's odyssey through picturesque vistas and vibrant markets reflects the timeless allure of discovery and the bonds that form along the way.

These stories, along with the many others in this collection, challenge the reader to see beyond the ordinary. They invite you to embark on vast and intimate journeys, to experience the myriad ways in which lives can intertwine, and to find beauty in the unexpected.

As you turn each page, let yourself be drawn into the worlds created by the authors. Allow their words to weave through your thoughts, to evoke laughter, tears, and reflection. This collection is more than just a series of stories; it is an invitation to dream, connect, and see the world through new eyes.

Within the digital echoes of "The Savvy Boys," you will find a profound exploration of how technology shapes our identities and legacies. The narrative delves into the heart of what it means to be human in an increasingly digital world, where the lines between the virtual and the real blur, and our creations take on lives of their own.

Meanwhile, "The Journey to Spain" will whisk you away on a sensory voyage through the heart of Europe. Through the eyes of Julien and Amélie, you will traverse the bustling streets of Paris, the serene paths of the Loire Valley, and the vibrant markets of Lyon. Their journey is not just one of physical travel, but also of inner discovery, as they forge a deep connection that transcends borders and backgrounds.

This collection offers myriad narratives, each a unique thread in the rich tapestry of human experience. From tales of love and loss to stories of triumph and trial, every piece invites contemplation and introspection. The authors have poured their hearts into these pages, creating worlds that are both fantastical and grounded in the universal truths of our existence.

As you delve into this anthology, you may find inspiration in the creativity and resilience of the characters. Let their stories remind you of the power of connection, the beauty in diversity, and the endless possibilities that lie within the human spirit. Welcome to this literary voyage. May it inspire you as deeply as it has the hearts and minds that crafted it.

Story 1: THE JOURNEY TO SPAIN

In the serene city of Geneva, nestled between mountains and lakes, lived Julien, an adventurer with a longing for Spain. With a backpack and journal, Julien set out through France's picturesque vistas. Along the cobblestone streets and rolling hills, he met Amélie, a traveler from Avignon with eyes like lavender fields and a radiant smile. Their serendipitous meeting felt like destiny.

Together, they explored Paris's boulevards, where fresh pastries mingled with street musicians' melodies. They shared stories under the ancient trees of the Loire Valley and laughed in Lyon's bustling markets. Each day brought new discoveries, and they documented their adventures under the stars each night. Their bond deepened, transforming their friendship into something profound.

Crossing into Spain, the warm breeze welcomed them. Their journey, filled with moments of joy and challenge, became a tapestry of shared dreams. In Spain, they found the inspiration they sought, dancing to flamenco rhythms, marveling at Barcelona's architecture, and watching Mediterranean sunsets. Their journey was a testament to the power of connection and the endless possibilities that unfold when two paths converge on the road less traveled.

The Journey to Spain

In Geneva, where mountains kiss the sky, lived Julien,
with a heart longing to fly.
An adventurer's soul, with dreams so grand,
He sought Spain's sun-drenched, golden land.

With a backpack packed and journal tight,
He ventured forth into the morning light.
Through France's cobblestones and rolling green,
His path led to a sight serene.

In Avignon, from a town so quaint,
Came Amélie, whose eyes did paint
The fields of lavender in her gaze,
And with her smile, she lit the haze.

Their meeting was the stars' sweet plan,
A journey shared, hand in hand.
Through Paris' streets and Loire's shade,
Their stories in the markets played.

Each day brought moments new and bright,
Their journals filled by starry night.
Julien and Amélie's bond grew strong,
In company where they belong.

To Spain they crossed, where breezes warm
Embraced them like a friend's form.
From Geneva's calm to France's heart,
Their journey stitched them part by part.

They danced in Spain to flamenco's beat,
In Barcelona's wonders found their feat.
Watched the sun set over the sea,
In their shared dreams, they found the key.

A testament to bonds and ties,
The endless paths where hope flies.
When two souls on life's road blend,
New possibilities never end.

Story 2: Walking in the Rain from Geneva to Spain

In the quiet streets of Geneva, raindrops fall,
Their rhythm echoing the traveler's heart.
He sets forth on a journey, seeking solace,
To distant lands where the sun kisses the sea.

Through the winding roads of France, he walks,
His footsteps leaving imprints on wet cobblestones.
And there, by chance, he meets her—
A girl as azure as the Mediterranean waves.

Her eyes hold secrets, depths unknown,
As if she emerged from the sea's hidden caverns.
Did he meet her on earth's surface, or perhaps,
In the fathomless depths beneath the waves?

They share stories under dripping umbrellas,
Of lost loves and forgotten promises.
He wonders if she carries memories too,
Of distant shores and whispered farewells.

But the rain cannot wash away their connection,
For it binds them like the threads of fate.
He leaves for Spain, promising to return,
To the same rainy streets of Geneva.

And when he does, the skies weep with joy,
As they reunite under the gray clouds.
Their love, like rain, knows no boundaries,
And memories merge with raindrops.

In the shadowed alleys, they dance,

Their laughter echoing through the mist.
He whispers, "Did I find you on land or sea?"
She smiles, "Perhaps both, in this rain-kissed twist."

Their hands touch, and time unravels,
As if the world conspired to bring them close.
He recalls their first meeting, her eyes like sapphire,
And how he longed for her when the rain ceased.

But life is a tempest, and separation inevitable.

He returns to Geneva, heart heavy with longing.
The streets remember their footsteps,
And the rain weeps for their lost moments.

Yet destiny has its own design,
One day, she stands before him, drenched.
Her smile, a sunbeam breaking through clouds,
And he knows: this is the reunion he sought.

They embrace, raindrops mingling with tears.
Her kiss tastes of salt and eternity.He whispers, "Did I
find you on earth or sea?"
She laughs, "In both realms, our love's infinity."

Story 3: Love for Nature

In the heart of the woods, where leaves sway and
whispers of the wind tell secrets, lived Ethan—a city

dweller by necessity but a nature lover at heart. Each weekend, he escaped the concrete jungle for the forest's embrace. One such weekend, deep in the woods, the golden sky mesmerized him. Beneath the canopy, he found serene solitude, feeling the rustling leaves' song and wandering not in fear but wonder.

Ethan reached a river, its pure rhythm reflecting the sky's vastness. Kneeling by the water, he marveled at its beauty as a life mirror. Climbing a mountain, its majesty testament to time, he stood at its peak, breathing crisp air, overwhelmed by reverence for the world.

As night fell, Ethan returned to his campsite. The fireflies' dance under the moon created a light symphony. Watching the stars guide the lost, he found peace in nature's beauty. The next morning, the wind's gentle caress and birds' dawn chorus cleansed his soul. The previous night's rustling leaves and crickets' song had been nature's lullaby.

Exploring further, Ethan observed animals in their habitat—marveling at the lion's roar, deer's grace, eagle's flight, and rabbit's hop. Each creature added to the wild's tapestry, where he found thrill and timelessness. One evening, gentle rain fell. Under the canopy, he felt the raindrops' rhythm and smelled the divine scent of petrichor. A rainbow across the sky filled him with profound joy and gratitude.

Nature's love became his guiding star, leading him to joy, peace, and purpose. Ethan discovered true harmony with the earth, making every element of nature his source of inspiration and peace.

Love of Nature Poem

In the heart of the woods, where the green leaves sway,
And the wind whispers secrets in a mystical way.
The sun paints the sky with hues of gold,
A spectacle of nature, bold and untold.

Beneath the canopy, where the shadows play,
In the silent serenity, I lose my way.
The rustling leaves sing a melodious song,
In nature's embrace, is where I belong.

The river's rhythm, so gentle and pure,
Its mesmerizing beauty, for which there's no cure.
Reflecting the sky, so vast and blue,
A mirror of life, ever-changing and true.

The mountain's majesty, standing tall and grand,
A testament to time, in a timeless land.
Cloaked in snow, or adorned with green,
A sight to behold, a sight unseen.

The dance of the fireflies, under the moon's glow,
A symphony of light, in the night's shadow.

The stars twinkle, like diamonds in the night,
Guiding the lost, with their gentle light.

In the love of nature, I find my peace,
In its timeless beauty, my worries cease.
From the break of dawn to the fall of night,
Nature's love is an endless delight.

The whispering wind, with its gentle caress,
In the heart of the forest, it's a sweet confess.
It carries the fragrance of the blooming flowers,
A scent so divine, in the twilight hours.

The chirping of birds, at the break of dawn,
A melody so pure, in the early morn.
They spread their wings, in the azure sky,
In the vast canvas, they freely fly.

The rustle of leaves, under the moon's beam,
In the quiet night, it's like a dream.
The crickets' song, in the cool night air,
Nature's lullaby, beyond compare.

The dew on the grass, in the morning light,
Like pearls shining, oh what a sight!
The beauty of nature, in every frame,
Each day is different, yet somehow the same.

In the love of nature, I find my joy,
Every sunrise, a new day to enjoy.
From the mountain's peak to the ocean's might,
In nature's wonder, I take delight.

The rhythm of the rain, on the windowpane,
A soothing symphony, a melodious refrain.
It washes away, the dust and the grime,
In every droplet, a moment in time.

The petrichor rises, from the thirsty earth,
Nature rejoices, in its rebirth.
Rainbow arcs, in the cloudy sky,
A painter's stroke, a feast for the eye.

In the love of nature, I find my solace,
In the rain's rhythm, a gentle grace.
From the sky's tears to the earth's delight,
In nature's cycle, a beautiful sight.

The changing seasons, in their endless dance,
Each one brings its own romance.
Spring's bloom, summer's heat,
Autumn's colors, winter's sleet.

Spring whispers life, in every bud and bloom,
After winter's sleep, it dispels the gloom.
Summer's sun, high and bright,
Long days of warmth, and starry night.

Autumn paints, with a golden brush,
In the cooling air, there's a tranquil hush.
Winter's touch, cold and white,
A blanket of snow, under the moonlight.

In the love of nature, I find my muse,
In the changing seasons, life renews.
From spring's promise to winter's night,
Nature's love is pure and bright.

The animals' chorus, in the heart of the wild,
Nature's children, innocent and mild.
The lion's roar, the deer's grace,
Each has its own, in this vast space.

The eagle's flight, so high and free,
In the open sky, it's a sight to see.
The rabbit's hop, in the green meadow,
In nature's book, each a unique shadow.

In the love of nature, I find my thrill,
In the animal's world, time stands still.
From the jungle's heart to the ocean's depth,

Nature's love, in every breath.

The ocean's waves, with their rhythmic beat,
A symphony of nature, so subtle and sweet.
The ebb and flow, the high and low,
In the moon's pull, they come and go.

The seashell's whisper, of tales untold,
Of sunken treasures, and pirates bold.
The salty breeze, the sandy shore,
Nature's love, forevermore.

In the love of nature, I find my song,
In the ocean's waves, I find where I belong.
From the sea's depth to the sky's height,

Nature's love, is my guiding light.
The moon's soft glow, in the velvet night,
A beacon of hope, a source of light.
The stars' twinkle, in the endless dark,
Each a story, each a spark.

The constellations, in their celestial dance,
In the universe's expanse, they prance.
The shooting star, a fleeting sight,
Nature's love, in the quiet night.

In the love of nature, I find my peace,
In the moon and stars, my wonder cease.

From the earth's core to the galaxies afar,
Nature's love is my guiding star.

Story 4: Love in an Isolated Island

In the shifting tides of reality and dreams, Najeeb found himself shipwrecked on an isolated Caribbean Isle. This untouched paradise, with verdant greenery and immaculate beaches, offered solace from the world's clamor. Awakening to waves and a golden sky, Jim felt a profound peace. Here, he could reconnect with nature.

Days turned into a tapestry of exploration. Dense forests, vibrant flowers, and diverse fauna filled Najeeb with wonder. One afternoon, he spotted a woman emerging from the sea. Her beauty was otherworldly, with golden hair and blue eyes. She introduced herself as Feuona, and an inexplicable bond formed between them.

Nathalie joined Najeeb in his solitude. Together, they explored the island's hidden wonders, diving into crystal waters and basking in the sun. Each day brought new adventures, painting their shared moments on nature's canvas. Their bond deepened, filling Jim with joy and happiness.

One starlit night, under a canopy of stars, Najeeb confessed his love. Feuona, moved by his words, kissed him, and their love felt as vast as the ocean. Days turned into weeks, and their love grew stronger. They found a secluded grove and planted a tree, symbolizing their growing love.

Reality eventually beckoned. Najeeb knew he couldn't stay on the island forever. With a heavy heart, he prepared to leave. Feuona reassured him, "Our love is strong and will endure. Follow your destiny, and know I will always be with you."

Embracing her one last time, Najeeb stepped into a boat, feeling sorrow mixed with hope. He embarked on a journey of self-discovery, learning from diverse cultures. Despite the distance, Feuona's love remained his guiding light.

Love's Guiding Star

In the moon and stars, my wonder cease,

From earth's core to galaxies afar,

Nature's love, a guiding star,

In isolated isles, love finds release.

Najeeb on a Caribbean shore,

Shipwrecked, finds peace once more,

Verdant greens and tranquil seas,

Nature's splendor sets his heart at ease.

Days of exploration, joy abound,

In forests deep, new wonders found,

Nathalie from the sea did rise,

With golden hair and sapphire eyes.

Together they roamed the island's grace,

In sunlit days and night's embrace,

A bond so deep, so pure, so true,

Their love, a garden endlessly grew.

One starlit night, love did confess,

In Nathalie's kiss, pure happiness,

A tree they planted, love's symbol strong,

In nature's song, their hearts belong.

But time's call, Najeeb must heed,

With heavy heart, he must proceed,

Nathalie's words, a hopeful plea,

"Our love endures, it sets you free."

Najeeb in dreams, an island lost,

In time and wonder, love embossed,

A paradise where hearts could glean,

Secrets only hearts could glean.

Nathalie's beauty, a golden hue,

With eyes reflecting bays of blue,

Her laughter's symphony, her spirit wild,

Najeeb's heart by her beguiled.

In twilight's glow, their stories shared,

In starry nights, their souls laid bare,

Nathalie's wisdom, a guiding light,

Her presence made each day bright.

Their bond grew strong, their love profound,

In every moment, joy was found,

A kiss beneath the moon's soft glow,

A promise sealed in love's flow.

But dreams must end, dawn's light proclaimed,

Yet in Najeeb's heart, love remained,

For in his verses, Nathalie's theme,

A poet's love, forever a dream.

In love's embrace, both near and far,

Najeeb and Nathalie found their star,

In nature's wonder, hearts set free,

Love's guiding light, eternally.

Story 5: Love in Wonder Island

In the realm of dreams, where thoughts take flight, there was an isolated island where Jim found himself lost in both time and wonder. This island, a paradise untouched by the chaos of the world, held secrets that only the heart could decipher. One day, as Jim wandered through its blooming gardens under the twilight's glow, he encountered a vision of beauty that seemed almost unreal.

Her hair was a cascade of golden sun rays, and her eyes reflected the serene azure of the bays. There was a deep and profound mystery in her gaze, where the sky seemed to find a home. Jim felt his heart strumming to an unknown melody, as if his very soul had been awakened.

This woman, Nada, moved with the grace of a gentle dove. Everything about her was exciting and new, like a morning kissed with dew. Her laughter was a sweet symphony, her presence a completion of every moment. In her, Jim discovered an eternal and deep love, a promise he intended to keep.

They spent days exploring the island, sharing stories and dreams under the starry sky. Nada's spirit was wild and free, her strength a majestic sight, her courage burning bright. She became Jim's muse, his source of truth and inspiration. Her voice was a melody that soothed his soul, and her words made him whole. Her wisdom was a guiding star, and her kindness was a light that reached both near and far.

Their bond grew stronger with each passing day, and Jim found in Nada a vision and a mission. Her smile, like the dawn's first light, brought him joy beyond measure. Together, they created memories woven like a tapestry, each moment a precious gem in the crown of their love.

One evening, as the sun dipped below the horizon, Nada and Jim shared their first kiss under the moon's soft glow. Her lips were like petals of a blooming rose, and his heart sang a symphony in her presence. The world around them seemed to fade, leaving only their beautiful serenade. A promise was sealed, a bond so deep, a memory they would forever keep.

Every sunrise and every nightfall, Jim's love for Nada outshone them all. Their walks in the park, their dances in the rain, their star-gazing sessions on clear nights—each memory was a testament to their enduring love.

But as the dawn broke and the stars began to fade, Jim realized that this enchanted island, this profound love, was a dream. Yet, in his heart, the dream remained. In every verse he wrote, in every refrain he sang, Na's essence lingered. In the end, it was but a poet's dream, a love woven into a lyrical theme.

In her, Jim found his theme. In her, he found his dream. And though he awoke to the world of reality, the love he discovered in that isolated island continued to shine brightly in his heart, guiding him like a star in the night sky.

Love in Wonder Island

In the realm of dreams, where thoughts take flight,
There exists a woman, a radiant light.
Her hair, a cascade of golden sun rays,
Her eyes, the azure of serene bays.

Her gaze, a mystery, deep and profound,
In her blue eyes, the sky is found.
A firm body, like a sculpted art,
Her beauty, a melody that strums the heart.

Everything about her, exciting and new,
Like a morning kissed with dew.
Her laughter, a symphony so sweet,
Her presence makes every moment complete.

Her grace, like a gentle dove,
In her, Jim found his love.
Her spirit, wild and free,
In her, Jim found his glee.

Her strength, a majestic sight,
Her courage, burning bright.
In her, Jim sees his muse,
In her, he finds his truth.

His love for her, eternal and deep,
A promise he intends to keep.
In every verse, in every line,
His love for her will forever shine.

Her voice, a melody that soothes the soul,
Her words make Jim whole.
Her wisdom, like a guiding star,
Her kindness felt both near and far.

Her smile, like the dawn's first light,
Her joy, the day's delight.
Her sorrow, the evening's gentle tear,
In her emotions, Jim is near.

Her dreams, like a soaring bird,
Her hopes, in every word.
In her, Jim sees a vision,
In her, he finds his mission.

His love for her, like a timeless song,
A melody where they both belong.
In every sunrise, in every night's fall,
His love for her outshines them all.

In her, Jim found his rhyme,
In her, he found his time.
In every beat, in every breath,
His love for her transcends even death.

In a garden blooming, under the twilight's glow,
Where the flowers whispered, and the gentle winds
blow.
Their eyes met, in that magical setting,
A moment in time, their hearts won't be forgetting.

Her golden hair, caught the sun's last light,
Her blue eyes sparkled brightly in the night.
A firm handshake, a smile so inviting,
In that moment, it was quite exciting.

His heart fluttered, like a bird in flight,
In her presence, everything felt right.
That first meeting, under the star's array,
In his heart, forever it will stay.

Their shared memories, like a woven tapestry,
Moments of joy, moments of ecstasy.
The walks in the park, under the autumn leaves,
The summer picnics, the springtime eves.

The laughter they shared, the tears they shed,
The dreams they dreamed, lying side by side in bed.
The silent whispers, in the still of the night,
The gentle kisses, in the morning light.

Their dances in the rain, their snowball fights,

Their star-gazing sessions, on clear nights.
Every memory, a precious gem,
In the crown of their love, each a shining emblem.

In her, Jim found his past,
In their memories, a love that will last.
In every shared smile, in every shared tear,
His love for her, crystal clear.

Their first kiss, under the moon's soft glow,
A moment frozen in time, a love beginning to grow.
Her lips, like petals of a blooming rose,
His heart, a symphony that in her presence, arose.

The world around them seemed to fade,
In that moment, a beautiful serenade.
A promise sealed, a bond so deep,
A memory they would forever keep.

His heart raced, his mind a whirl,
In that kiss, he found his world.
In her, Jim found his bliss,
In the magic of their first kiss.

In the realm of dreams, where thoughts take flight,
A poet's imagination, in the still of the night.
A beautiful woman, a love so profound,
In his verses, their story is found.

But as the dawn breaks, and the stars fade,
The poet awakens, and the dream begins to wade.
Yet in his heart, the dream remains,
In every verse, in every refrain.
For in the end, it's but a poet's dream,
A love woven in a lyrical theme.
In her, Jim found his theme,
In her, he found his dream.

Story 6: Story 6: Deep in the Ocean

In bustling New York, John was a prominent fintech executive, known for his sharp mind. However, beneath the suit, he harbored a passion for the ocean, sparked by childhood tales of underwater kingdoms and sea creatures. As he grew, this fascination deepened. He mastered diving, studied marine biology, and discovered he could communicate with marine life.

John made a life-changing decision to leave his job and devote himself to ocean exploration. He moved to a coastal town to be closer to the sea, diving daily to explore its depths and communicate with its inhabitants. He discovered new species, uncovered hidden treasures, and solved ocean mysteries. The peace he found underwater contrasted sharply with city life, giving him a profound sense of belonging.

John's story spread, inspiring others to pursue their passions. He became an ocean guardian and friend to sea creatures, his love for the ocean as vast as its waters. Through his adventures, he reminded others that it's never too late to change paths.

John's journey led to memorable encounters with sea creatures, deepening his connection with the ocean. His new life was a testament to his enduring passion and commitment to the wonders of the underwater world. His exploration became a beacon of inspiration, showing the power of following one's true calling.

Deep in The Ocean

In the heart of the city, amidst the concrete and glass,
Lived John, a man of class.
But his heart yearned for something more,
A love he found on the ocean floor.

He traded his suit, his tie, his life,
For the ocean's call, free from strife.
With each dive, with each breath,
He found a love stronger than death.

He spoke to the creatures, he touched the plants,
In the ocean's depth, he found his chance.
From the city's noise, from the corporate race,
He found peace in the ocean's embrace.

The dolphins danced, the whales did sing,
In John's heart, the ocean did ring.
Beneath the waves, under the sea's might,
John found his heart's delight.

His love for the ocean, as deep as the sea,
Set his spirit, his soul, free.
In the water's embrace, in the sea's vast sprawl,
Lives the tale of John.

in the face of storms, under the thunder's call,
John stood firm, he stood tall.
The waves roared, the sea did churn,
Yet from the challenge, John did not turn.

He embraced the storm, he faced the tide,
In the ocean's challenge, he took pride.

For each storm passed, each challenge met,
Made his love for the ocean, a stronger bet.

Under the moonlit nights, beneath the starry skies,
John found beauty, where the sea meets the eyes.
The stars reflected on the ocean's face,
In the serene nights, he found his place.

The moonlight danced on the gentle waves,
Illuminating the sea's hidden caves.
In the quiet of the night, under the stars' glow,
John's love for the ocean continued to grow.

In the coastal town, under the sun's warm glow,
John found a home, with the sea below.
A city man no more, in the town he did reside,
With the ocean by his side, in the tide's gentle glide.

His love for the ocean, as constant as the northern star,
Remained in his heart, no matter where he is.
A citizen of the town, a friend of the sea,
In the ocean's embrace, John was forever free.

Story 7: MY OCEAN LOVE!

In the heart of the bustling city, amidst the concrete
and glass, lived John, a man known for his impeccable

class and sharp intellect. By day, he donned a suit and tie, navigating the corridors of power in a prominent Fintech company. But beneath the polished exterior, John's heart yearned for something more—a love he found in the depths of the ocean.

John's fascination with the sea began in his childhood, nurtured by tales of underwater kingdoms and mysterious sea creatures. As he grew older, this fascination turned into a profound love. He spent every spare moment learning about the ocean, mastering the art of diving, and even studying marine biology. With its relentless pace and noise, the corporate world felt increasingly distant as John's passion for the ocean grew.

One pivotal day, John made a life-changing decision. He traded his suit, tie, and high-profile job for the call of the ocean. His colleagues were shocked, unable to comprehend his choice. But John knew in his heart that he was following his true calling.

He moved to a quaint coastal town, where the ocean was his new neighbor. Every day, he would dive into the azure waters, exploring the ocean's depths and communing with its inhabitants. He spoke to the dolphins, danced with the whales, and touched the vibrant corals. In the ocean's embrace, John found a peace and fulfillment he had never experienced before.

Beneath the waves, John discovered a world teeming with life and beauty. The dolphins danced joyfully around him, their playful clicks and whistles creating a melody that resonated in his heart. The majestic whales sang hauntingly beautiful songs, filling John with a sense of awe and wonder. With each dive, his love for the ocean grew deeper, setting his spirit free.

John's connection to the ocean was not without its challenges. He faced fierce storms and roaring waves, but he stood firm, embracing the tempest with unwavering resolve. Each challenge met and overcome made his love for the ocean stronger. Under the moonlit nights and starry skies, John found beauty and solace. The moonlight danced on the gentle waves, illuminating hidden caves and reflecting the stars on the ocean's surface.

In the coastal town, John found a new home. He was no longer a city man but a citizen of the sea. Initially curious about the city man who had left it all behind, the locals grew to admire and respect him. They saw John's dedication to the ocean and his efforts to protect its fragile ecosystem. He became a beloved community member, known as a friend of the sea.

John's love for the ocean was as constant as the northern star. It guided him, bringing purpose and joy to his life. In the ocean's embrace, he was forever free. The rhythm of the tides, the sea song, and the waves' tranquility became his life's symphony.

Through his journey, John found his heart's delight. His love for the ocean was not just a passion but a testament to the transformative power of following one's true calling. In the water's vast expanse, he found his place, his peace, and his purpose. And so, the tale of John, the man who found love deep in the ocean, continues to inspire those who seek to follow their dreams and find their own heart's delight.

My Ocean Love

Beneath the city's hustle, in the heart so pure,
Lived a man named John, his love for the ocean so sure.
From the suit and tie; to the sea's vast expanse,
He traded skyscrapers for waves, in the ocean's dance.

A language he learned, of the creatures and plants,
In the ocean's depth, he found his chance.
He left the corporate world, its noise, and its strife,
For the whispering waves, a new life.

In the coastal town, by the sea so blue,
John found his calling, his passion anew.
With the dolphins he danced, with the whales he did glide,
In the ocean's embrace, he took in stride.

The octopus wise, the turtles so grand,
In the ocean's song, he found a new land.
The bioluminescent symphony, a sight to behold,
In the water world, John's story unfold.

From the city to the sea, a journey so bold,
John's love for the ocean, a tale to be told.
In the heart of the sea, his spirit set free,
John, the ocean's melody.

In the ocean's depth, where the sunlight fades,
John found secrets in the underwater glades.
With each dive he took, with each stroke he swam,
He unraveled the ocean's whispers, a beautiful exam.

From the coral reefs; to the sandy floor,
He explored the sea, always craving for more.

In the water's embrace, under the moon's soft glow,
John found his peace, in the ebb and flow.

His heart echoed the waves, his soul sang the sea's
song,
In the ocean's vastness, John found where he belongs.
A symphony of life, a ballet of light,
In the heart of the ocean, John's delight.

Story 8: The Guardian of Marbella: Pedro's Triumph

In the heart of Marbella, under the bright sun, lived Pedro, a man of wisdom and strength. Pedro was a shrewd businessman, known for his Midas touch. But beyond his business acumen, his greatest love was for his mother. She guarded an ancient artifact, the Eye of Marbella, symbolizing peace and prosperity. Pedro had vowed to protect this sacred object with his life.

One day, a greedy man sought the power of the Eye. Dark clouds loomed over Marbella as this man, driven by avarice, tried to claim the artifact. But Pedro, guided by his mother's wisdom, stood firm. His resolve never wavered. With a mind as sharp as his spirit, Pedro undertook the challenge.

A battle of wits ensued, a test of intellect and determination. Pedro, with his unyielding resolve and clever strategies, outsmarted the greedy man, leaving him far behind. The Eye of Marbella was safe, and the city breathed a collective sigh of relief. Pedro's victory echoed through the mountains and across the sea, a testament to his bravery and love for his city.

Betrayal and risk were constant companions, but Pedro faced them with a spirit that soared above adversity. His love for his mother, the city's protector, and his respect for her profound wisdom made him a hero. An inspiring director, Pedro's story of bravery and resilience unfolded as a tale of a son so dear, and a city saved from impending doom.

Pedro's legend bloomed in Marbella's heart, under the sun so bright. He became a beacon of hope, dispelling the gloom that once threatened their peaceful life. Even in the face of danger, Pedro stood tall, his courage unwavering. He answered the call to protect his beloved city with all his might.

The cunning businessman, blinded by greed, underestimated Pedro's strength and determination. With a heart full of love and a bright mind, Pedro outmaneuvered him repeatedly. Trials and tribulations came and went, but Pedro's spirit never dimmed. Each challenge met with his mother's love as his guiding light.

Pedro's story of bravery, told far and near, became a source of inspiration. His love for his mother, pure and true, gave him the strength to persevere. Deep respect for her wisdom was evident in every action he took. His journey was a testament to the power of love and the strength it brings.

So, here's to Pedro, a son so brave, who saved his city and protected the symbol of peace. His legend rings in the heart of Marbella, a testament to love and the joy it can bring. Pedro's triumph, born from love and wisdom, remains a shining example of courage and resilience. His legacy endures, a beacon of hope for generations to come.

The Guardian of Marbella: Pedro's Triumph Poem

In Marbella's heart, under the sun so bright,
Lived Pedro, a man of wisdom and might.

A businessman shrewd, with a Midas touch,
His love for his mother meant so much.

An ancient artifact, the Eye of Marbella,
His mother guarded, a secret to tell.
A symbol of peace, prosperity's key,
Pedro vowed to protect it, for all to see.

A greedy man sought the Eye's power,
Dark clouds over Marbella began to tower.
Pedro stood firm, his resolve never shook,
With his mother's guidance, the challenge he
undertook.

A battle of wits, a test of the mind,
Pedro outsmarted the man, leaving him behind.
The artifact was safe, the city breathed free,
Pedro's victory echoed, from mountain to sea.

Betrayal and risk, challenges galore,
Pedro faced them all, his spirit did soar.
His love for his mother, his city's protector,
Made him a hero, an inspiring director.

So, here's the tale of Pedro, a son so brave,
A story of love, and the city he saved.
In Marbella's heart, his legend does bloom,
A beacon of hope, dispelling the gloom.

In the face of danger, Pedro stood tall,
His courage unwavering, he answered the call.
With his mother's wisdom, his guiding light,
He fought for Marbella, with all his might.

The businessman cunning, with power and greed,
Underestimated Pedro didn't take heed.
With a heart full of love, and a mind so bright,
Pedro outsmarted him, with all his might.

Through trials and tribulations, Pedro did tread,
With his mother's love, he was led.
His story of bravery, it did unfold,
A tale of a hero, brave and bold.

His love for his mother, pure and true,
Gave him strength, saw him through.
His respect for her, deep and profound,
In his actions, it was found.

So, here's to Pedro, a son so dear,
His story of love, far and near.
In the heart of Marbella, his legend does ring,
A testament to love, and the joy it can bring.

Story 9: The Desert Storm

A boy named Mustafa was born in the heart of Jerusalem under the scorching desert sun. His early years were marred by the ravages of war, but hope never abandoned him. As a young man, he migrated to Jordan, where life began to show promise. With dreams in his eyes and a diploma in his hand, he ventured to Europe, landing in the vibrant streets of France.

In France, Mustafa worked odd jobs while studying finance. Despite the struggles, he remained hopeful. As the Parisian lights shimmered one fateful night, he met Mariam, a woman of captivating beauty and radiant spirit. Together, they danced through the night, their hearts intertwined. They married and soon welcomed a daughter named Amal. Life presented challenges, but love remained their guiding force.

Mustafa's career flourished. Starting from a humble bank job, he climbed the ladder with remarkable talent and flair, earning the nickname "Mr. Desert Storm" for his relentless drive and resilience. Yet, behind every storm stood Mariam, his calming force. Her unwavering support and love guided him through the highs and lows of his journey.

Retirement did not mark an end but the beginning of new adventures. With Mariam by his side, they traveled the world, each destination adding a piece to the tapestry of their memories. From Tokyo's cherry blossoms to Rome's ancient art, they embraced life's beauty together. They shared meals, drinks, and Cuban cigars under moonlit skies, cherishing each moment.

Mustafa, a chess player, painter, and lover of life, found fulfillment in every role he embraced. He was a dedicated banker, a devoted husband, a proud father, and a loving partner to Mariam. His story, a blend of fiction and truth, became a testament to resilience, love, and eternal youth. Mustafa and Mariam's love story continued to inspire through life's storms and calm, a bright beacon of hope.

The Desert Storm Poem

In the heart of Jerusalem, under the desert sun,
Was born a man named Mustafa, his journey just begun.
War-torn were his early years, yet hope was never gone,
To Jordan he migrated, and life moved on.

With dreams in his eyes, and a diploma in his hand,
He ventured to Europe, to the French land.
Working odd jobs, studying finance, he made his way,
And in the midst of it all, he found love one day.

Mariam was her name, a beauty so bright,
Together they danced, in the Parisian night.
A daughter they had, Amal was her name,
Life was challenging, but love was their game.

From a humble bank job to the Vice President's chair,
Mustafa climbed the ladder with talent and flair.
"Mr. Desert Storm", they called him with pride,
For he was a storm, taking life in stride.

But behind every storm, there's a calming force,
Mariam was his, guiding his course.
With love and support, she stood by his side,
In every high tide, she was his guide.

Retirement came, but not the end,
For life had more, around the bend.
With Mariam by his side, and love in their heart,
They traveled the world, making each place a part.

From Tokyo's cherry blossoms to Rome's ancient art,
Each city, each memory, a piece of their heart.
Food, drinks, and Cuban cigars,
Underneath the moon, and beneath the stars.

A chess player, a painter, a lover of life,
A dedicated banker, a husband, a father, and a loving
wife.
Mustafa's story, a blend of fiction and truth,
A tale of resilience, love, and eternal youth.

Story 10: Amin's Universe

In the heart of Marbella, under the starry night, lived a young man named Amin, whose dreams always took flight. With his modest telescope, he gazed at the sky, finding solace and inspiration in the vast cosmic ocean above.

"I love the universe, the galaxies so wide," Amin would whisper to himself, yearning for the cosmos with stars as his guide. To him, Earth seemed so small in the grand cosmic race. "Oh, how I wish," he'd sigh, "space could be my place."

One night, a comet appeared, a celestial delight that made Amin's heart flutter with joy. Its radiant tail painted the night sky, a beacon of his dreams guiding him closer to the cosmic light. For Amin, the comet symbolized hope and the promise of a brighter future beyond the stars.

As he watched the comet's journey across the celestial dome, Amin couldn't help but reflect on the wars and injustices that plagued Earth. In the vast cosmos, these troubles seemed distant and insignificant. "Is it worth it?" Amin wondered, his love for the universe growing with each year. The comet's passage reminded him of his dream of making space his home. "One day," he whispered under the starry sheen, "I will be among you, in the cosmic scene."

In the town of Marbella, where the sea meets the sand, Amin's love for the universe was a grand tale. His dreams, like comets, darted through the cosmos, etched deep in his heart. "Look beyond," he urged the townsfolk, "there's nothing to fear at the cosmic ballet. The universe is our home, our destiny, our part. Let's embrace the cosmos, let's make a start."

The comet's tail, like a brush on the night's canvas, painted a path for Amin, without any fuss. "Follow your dreams," it seemed to impart, "to the edge of the universe, and into its heart."

So, here's to Amin, a dreamer so bold, with a love for the universe, a sight to behold. May his journey continue under the star's gleam, in the vast cosmic ocean where dreamers dream. And in every starry night, may Amin find his home, in the space of his dream.

Amin`s Universe Poem

In the heart of Marbella, under the starry night,
Lives a young man named Amin, with dreams taking flight.
With his modest telescope, he gazes at the sky,
In the vast cosmic ocean, his dreams lie.

"I love the universe, the galaxies so wide,
I yearn for the cosmos, with stars as my guide.
The Earth seems so small, in the grand cosmic race,
Oh, how I wish, space could be my place."

A comet appears, a celestial delight,
Amin's heart flutters, at the beautiful sight.
It's a symbol of his dreams, a beacon in the night,
Guiding him closer, to the cosmic light.

Wars and injustice, on Earth they reside,
But in the vast cosmos, they cannot hide.
"Is it worth it?" Amin wonders, looking at the blue sphere,

His love for the universe, growing each year.

The comet's journey, across the celestial dome,
Reminds Amin of his dream, of making space his home.
"One day," he whispers, under the starry sheen,
"I will be among you, in the cosmic scene."

So, here's to Amin, and his love so bright,
For the universe, the stars, and the cosmic night.
May his dreams take flight, in the cosmic stream,
And may he find his home, in the space of his dream.

In the town of Marbella, where the sea meets the sand,
Amin's love for the universe, a tale so grand.
His dreams, like comets, through the cosmos they dart,
His love for the universe, etched deep in his heart.

"Look beyond," he whispers, to the townsfolk so dear,
"At the cosmic ballet, there's nothing to fear.
The universe is our home, our destiny, our part,
Let's embrace the cosmos, let's make a start."

The comet's tail, like a brush on the night's canvas,
Paints a path for Amin, without any fuss.
"Follow your dreams," it seems to impart,
"To the edge of the universe, and into its heart."

So, here's to Amin, a dreamer so bold,
With a love for the universe, a sight to behold.

May his journey continue, under the star's gleam,
In the vast cosmic ocean, where dreamers dream.

Story 11: The River of Life

In the heart of a verdant valley, nestled between towering mountains and stretching toward the vast sea, flowed the River of Life. With its divine purpose, this river carried the water of life, nourishing the earth on its unyielding journey. Its course, unwavering and true, never reversed.

The people of the valley, grateful for this divine gift, often gathered by the riverbanks to give thanks to the Creator. They knew the river was more than just a body of water; it was a source of life and sustenance. Its gentle murmur echoed a divine promise, quenching their thirst and making their crops grow.

One night, as the moon cast a silver glow on the river's surface, an elder named Elara stood by the banks, reflecting on the river's ancient wisdom. The moon's reflection in the tranquil waters seemed to connect time and space, a celestial mirror of the heavens. Elara whispered a prayer of gratitude, knowing the river's ceaseless flow was a testament to the Creator's might, bringing life and joy to the valley.

Rivers, the ancient highways, had long carried people and goods from dawn till noon. Boats and barges glided on the river's wide surface, a lifeline for trade. The river transported more than just goods; it carried stories and civilizations, its silent depths witnessing the rise and fall of human endeavors.

In ancient times, people revered the rivers, counting them as seven gifts from the gods. These blessings in liquid form were gratefully received, bringing life and abundance to all they touched. The river's sacred waters provided solace and courage, and the ancients whispered in awe, "Rivers are heaven's gift, a divine benevolence."

As Elara stood by the river, she remembered the wisdom of the ancients. She knew that protecting the rivers was safeguarding the very essence of life. With a heart full of reverence, she vowed to join the endeavor to protect these divine gifts now and forever.

Elara's commitment to the river inspired the valley's inhabitants. They rallied together, forming a community dedicated to preserving and protecting their cherished river. They understood that as long as the rivers flowed, life would not cease. In their eternal journey, the people found peace.

By day, they tended to the riverbanks, ensuring the waters remained clear and unpolluted. By night, they marveled at the moonlit reflections, a reminder of the river's celestial connection. The river's rhythm became their own, its flow a symbol of life's continuity.

Generations passed, but the river's significance never waned. The people of the valley continued to honor their divine gift, passing down stories of the river's life-sustaining power. In their collective memory, the River of Life remained a source of inspiration, a testament to the enduring bond between humanity and nature.

And so, the tale of the River of Life continued, its waters carrying the hopes and dreams of all who revered its sacred flow. The people of the valley, guided by the wisdom of the ancients, stood united in their mission to protect the river, ensuring that life would flourish along its banks for generations to come.

The River of Life Poem

In the grand tapestry of life, rivers flow with a divine purpose,
Carrying the water of life, their course they never reverse.
From the highest mountains to the vast sea,
They nourish the earth, in their journey free.

We thank the Creator, for this gift so grand,
For the rivers that crisscross the land.
They quench our thirst, they make the crops grow,
In their gentle murmur, a divine echo.

Oh, the creator, to you we bow,
For the rivers of life, we thank you now.
Their ceaseless flow, a testament to your might,
Bringing life and joy, making our world bright.

So, here's to the rivers, and to the life they sustain,
May we protect them, with all our might and main.
For as long as rivers flow, life will not cease,
In their eternal journey, we find our peace.

In the still of the night, under the moon's gentle glow,
The river carries a silver light, in its steady flow.
A mirror to the celestial orb, in its tranquil grace,
The moon's reflection in the river, time, and space
embrace.

Rivers, the ancient highways, under the sun and the
moon,
Carrying people and goods, from the break of dawn till
noon.
Boats and barges glide, on their surface so wide,
A lifeline for trade, with the flowing tide.

From the smallest village to the bustling town,
Rivers carry life's rhythm, up and down.
People, goods, stories, they transport all,
In their silent depths, civilizations rise and fall.

In ancient times, under the vast blue heaven,
Rivers were revered, their number counted as seven.
Gifts from the gods, so the ancients believed,
Blessings in liquid form, gratefully received.

From the heavens they flow, to the earth below,
Bringing life and abundance, making everything grow.
A divine gift, in every ripple and wave,
In their sacred waters, the people found solace and
brave.

The ancients whispered, in awe and reverence,
"Rivers are heaven's gift, a divine benevolence."
So, let's honor their wisdom, let's join the endeavor,
To protect our rivers, now and forever.

Story 12: Love for my Homeland!

In the heart of a land kissed by the sun, beneath a sky so wide, lived Amir. His homeland was a tapestry of rolling hills, lush valleys, and grand fields, a place that held his heart in an unbreakable bond. The language they spoke was like music, clear and sweet, filling the air with melody. The songs they sang, the stories they told, and the bonds they shared were treasures Amir carried with him everywhere.

As fate would have it, Amir found himself far from his beloved land, in a foreign place where the customs and language were different. Yet, the love for his homeland never left him. The memories of its festive cheer, the mouthwatering food, and the vibrant music remained vivid in his dreams. His heart yearned for his homeland's embrace, the sun's warmth, and the gentle murmur of the fields.

The love for his country was woven into his very being, as essential as the blood flowing through his veins. Through every triumph and trial, this love remained steadfast, a guiding star in his life. No matter the distance, Amir knew that he would always return to his homeland, a place that was forever his home.

Amir's heart expanded with pride and joy, his soul resonating with the love for his beautiful homeland. It was a love that transcended time and space, a love that would forever be a beacon of hope and belonging in his life. And so, Amir's story was one of deep connection and unwavering loyalty to the land that shaped him, a testament to the enduring power of love for one's homeland.

Love for My Homeland Poem

In the heart of the land where I was born,
Under the sky so wide and the sun so warm.
The hills, the valleys, the fields so grand,
Oh, how I love my beautiful homeland.

The language we speak, so sweet and clear,
The songs we sing, so dear to my ear.
The tales we tell, the bonds we share,
In my heart, I carry them everywhere.

Far away, in a foreign place,
I long for my homeland's embrace.
The food, the music, the festive cheer,
In my dreams, I hold them near.

The love for my country, strong and deep,
In my heart, forever it will keep.
Like the blood that flows in my veins,
It's a love that never wanes.

Through the good times and the strife,
It's the love of my life.
For my homeland, I'll always yearn,
To my homeland, I'll always return.

No matter where I roam,
My homeland will always be my home.
With pride and joy, my heart expands,
For the love of my beautiful homeland.

Story 13: Our Love of the Sea!

In the heart of every man, woman, and child lies a profound love for the ocean, deep and wild. This love, born of gratitude, respect, and awe, is evident in the life the ocean gives to all. The vast and deep ocean harbors secrets and wonders within its depths.

From the highest mountains to the widest seas, the ocean brought forth a bountiful feast, nourishing human, bird, and beast alike. Fish of every shape and hue and crustaceans and mollusks provided rich sustenance from the ocean's briny embrace. And from its treasure trove, came pearls and corals, gleaming bright under the moon's soft light, enchanting all who beheld them.

The ocean also served as a wide and free highway connecting lands across the sea. It carried goods from shore to shore, fostering the exchange of cultures and the exploration of new worlds. Whenever respite was needed, people retreated to the ocean's shores, where the sound of waves and salty air lifted their spirits from despair.

Deep within the ocean's belly, black as night, lay oil and gas reserves, vital for fueling flights and journeys. It's clear and cool waters provided drinking water, a precious jewel that sustained life.

The coastal town's love for the ocean was palpable. Its freely given gifts were cherished and revered. The ocean's ceaseless flow and boundless beauty made it an eternal part of their lives. The people were forever grateful for all that the ocean gave, knowing that their love for the ocean would live on, deep in their hearts.

Our Sea Love Poem

In the heart of every man, woman, and child,
Lies a love for the ocean, so deep and wild.
A love born of gratitude, respect, and awe,
For the ocean gives us life, this we saw.

The ocean, so vast, so deep and wide,
A world of wonder, with secrets inside.
From its depths, it brings forth a feast,
For human, bird, and beast.

Fish of every shape and hue,
Crustaceans and mollusks too,
Providing protein, rich and fine,
From the ocean's briny brine.

And from the ocean's treasure trove,
Comes jewelry that we love.
Pearls and corals, gleaming bright,
In the ocean's soft moonlight.

The ocean, a highway wide and free,
Connecting lands across the sea.
Carrying goods from shore to shore,
Bringing cultures to explore.

And when we seek a respite sweet,
To the ocean's shores, we retreat.
The sound of waves, the salty air,
Lifts our spirits from despair.

Deep in its belly, black as night,
Lies oil and gas, to fuel our flight.
And from its waters, clear and cool,
We draw forth drinking water, a precious jewel.

So, here's to the ocean, deep and wide,
Our love for you, we cannot hide.
For all the gifts you freely give,
In our hearts, you'll forever live.

Story 14: My Beloved Green Mountain

In the heart of Libya, under the sun's golden beam, lay the majestic Green Mountain, a place revered for its beauty and fertility. This mountain, a dream of paradise, stretched across fertile lands and basked in the gleam of the Mediterranean. It was a haven that captured the world's esteem.

Under Apollo's light, the slopes of the Green Mountain teemed with thriving crops. Athena's wisdom echoed in every stream, and Poseidon's blessing graced the seam where the sea met the land. Demeter's touch made the land supreme, ensuring its bounty and splendor.

At the heart of this paradise stood the ancient city of Cyrene, proud and tall, echoing history's themes. The courage of Omer Al Mukhtar resounded in the valleys, a beacon of freedom that inspired all. The mountain's summer beauty was a sight to behold, like a beautiful dream come to life.

The eastern people, living by the mountain's stream, found joy and peace in its serene regime. The prophecy of prosperity filled their hearts with hope, making their eyes gleam with anticipation. Under the moon's gentle beam, the Green Mountain stood as a symbol of love, an integral part of their lives.

This love, like a flowing stream, was deep and enduring, holding a special esteem in the hearts of the people. The Green Mountain was more than just a geographic feature; it was a testament to their struggle, their fight, and their history.

To the strong and bright youth of Libya, the mountain called in the moon's soft light. It was a gift from the Creator, a majestic sight to cherish and protect. The future of Green Mountain lay in their hands, a treasure to guard day and night.

As generations passed, the love for the Green Mountain was a legacy handed down. Under the old fig tree, children learned of its beauty and history. They felt the wind, saw the majesty, and understood the profound love that flowed through every tree.

The people of Libya made a promise, a guarantee to love the mountain for eternity. As long as the sun rose and the sea existed, the Green Mountain's love would forever be. It was more than a mountain; it was their birthright, their heritage, a symbol of their enduring spirit.

My Beloved Green Mountain Poem

In the heart of Libya, under the sun's golden beam,
Lies my beloved, the majestic Green Mountain's dream.
With its fertile lands and the Mediterranean's gleam,
It's a paradise, a heaven, in the world's esteem.

Apollo's light bathes its slopes, making the crops teem,
Athena's wisdom echoes in every stream.
Poseidon's blessing graces the sea's seam,
And Demeter's touch makes the land supreme.

The city of Cyrene, where history's theme,
Stands proud and tall, in the past's gleam.
Omer Al Mukhtar's courage, like a beam,
Resounds in the valleys, in freedom's scream.

The mountain's beauty, in the summer's gleam,
Is a sight to behold, like a beautiful dream.
The eastern people, by the mountain's stream,
Find joy and peace, in its serene regime.

The prophecy of prosperity, like a beam,
Fills our hearts with hope, makes our eyes gleam.
The Green Mountain, under the moon's beam,
Is a symbol of love, a part of our theme.

My love for the mountain, like a flowing stream,
Is deep and enduring, a constant theme.
In my heart, it holds a special esteem,
The Green Mountain, my love, my dream.

To the youth of Libya, strong and bright,
The Green Mountain calls, in the moon's soft light.
A gift from the creator, a majestic sight,
A treasure to cherish, with all your might.

Nurture its lands, keep its waters bright,
In your hands lies the power, the might.
The mountain's future, in your sight,
Guard it, protect it, day, and night.

Remember, the mountain's not just height,
It's a symbol of our struggle, our fight.
In its green expanse, in its majestic flight,
Lies the story of Libya, in every rite.

So, rise, youth of Libya, rise to the height,
The Green Mountain calls, in the star's light.
Love it, protect it, with all your might,
For it's not just a mountain, it's our birthright.

To the children of tomorrow, hear our plea,
The Green Mountain's love, as vast as the sea.
A legacy of our ancestors, a decree,
To love and protect, for eternity.

Teach your children, under the old fig tree,
Of the mountain's beauty, its history.
Let them feel the wind, let them see,
The Green Mountain's love, wild and free.

Pass down the stories, in every degree,
Of Apollo's light, of Athena's decree.
Let them know, let them see,

The Green Mountain's love, in every tree.

So, here's our promise, our guarantee,
To love the mountain, for eternity.
For as long as the sun rises, as long as the sea,
The Green Mountain's love will forever be.

Story 15: THE ETERNAL LOVE

In the oldest city, bathed in the sun's golden rays, a beautiful girl named Layla was born. Raised with care and love under her father's gentle guidance, she grew up free like a bird in May. Life, however, took a turn when she was married young to a man not of her choosing. She bore him sons, yet love was missing from their life, casting a gray shadow over her early days.

Determined to find her own path, Layla left for London to learn and discover herself. Returning to her homeland with a heart still seeking, she met a handsome man who proposed without delay. Breaking norms, she said yes, embracing love in her own way.

Their connection sparked instantly, a soul's ballet dancing in the city of lights. "I knew you from a thousand years away," she said, and he smiled, replying, "Yes, in another life, in another day." Years passed without a word until fate led them to Montreux, to the serene bay where their love rekindled like the sun's first ray. They married, their love stronger than the Milky Way.

Struggles came, but together they stayed, their eternal love shining brighter each day. In his arms, Layla found her true way, her first and only love in life's grand play. Their love story, a beacon's ray, became a testament to love that would never fray, an eternal love that would always stay in their hearts, forever and a day.

Under the moon's soft glow and the stars' array, their love blossomed quietly in the bay. The celestial bodies, in their silent ballet, witnessed their love night and day. Their laughter echoed in Montreux's alleyway, a melody of joy and a symphony's play. The town listened to their love's relay, a testament of love that would never sway.

By the lake, under the stars' dove, their love reflected, a mirror of love. The water shimmered like a treasure trove, mirroring their love as pure as a dove. As the sun set and the night unwove, their love story, like a treasure trove, echoed in Montreux, in every cove—an eternal tale of their undying love.

Here's to Layla and her beloved, to their love and the moon above. Their love story, fitting like a glove, remains an eternal tale of undying love. Their legacy lived on, inspiring others to believe in the power and beauty of true love that transcends time and space

Eternal Love

In the oldest city, under the sun's golden ray,
A beautiful girl was born, to love and to play.
Raised with care, in her father's gentle sway,
She grew up free, like a bird in the May.

Married young, to a man not of her say,
She bore him sons, in her life's early day.
But love was missing, in their life's gray,
So, she chose to leave, to find her own way.

To London she traveled, to learn, to assay,
Returned to her homeland, in her heart a gentle fray.
A handsome man proposed, without delay,
She said yes, breaking norms, in her own way.

In the city of lights, a man did lay,
A connection sparked, in their soul's ballet.
"I knew you," she said, "from a thousand years' away."
He smiled, "Yes, in another life, in another day."

Years passed, no words to say,
Until in Montreux, fate led them to the bay.
Their love rekindled, like the sun's first ray,
They married; their love stronger than the Milky Way.

Struggles came, but together they stay,
Their eternal love, shining brighter each day.

In his arms, she found her true way,
Her first, her only love, in life's grand play.

Their love story, a beacon's ray,
A testament to love, that will never fray.
An eternal love, that will always stay,
In their hearts, forever and a day.

Under the moon's soft glow, and the stars' array,
Their love blossomed, in the quiet of the bay.
The celestial bodies, in their silent ballet,
Witnessed their love, night, and day.

Their laughter echoed, in Montreux's alleyway,
A melody of joy, a symphony's play.
The town listened, to their love's relay,
A testament of love, that will never sway.

By the lake, under the stars' dove,
Their love reflected, a mirror of love.
The water shimmered, like a treasure trove,
Mirroring their love, as pure as a dove.

As the sun sets, and the night unwove,
Their love story, like a treasure trove,
Echoes in Montreux, in every cove,
An eternal tale, of their undying love.

So, here's to them, to their love,
To the moon above, to the cooing dove.
Their love story, fits like a glove,
An eternal tale, of their undying love.

Story 16: Environment Forever Love

The gods resided in the heart of the cosmos and looked concerned about Earth. "Look at the humans," Zeus thundered, his eyes wide with worry. They've lost their way and forgotten to sway with nature."

Descending to Earth, the gods took human forms, blending seamlessly into the world below. They brought wisdom and lessons and were determined to teach humanity the love for nature that lay within reach. Zeus spoke first, "Respect the Earth, your home, for from its bounty, you have grown."

Athena followed, "Use resources with care; remember, it's a duty we all share." Poseidon roared next, "Keep the waters clean, for life it nurtures, in unseen ways."

Demeter whispered softly, "Let the soil be, for it gives life to tree and bee." Ares, with a stern gaze, challenged, "Change your ways, or face defeat."

The humans listened and learned, realizing the value of nature and their own worth. Hermes, the cunning messenger, devised a test. He offered humanity a machine of destruction, but they chose nature, cherishing it like a precious gem.

Through trials and time, humans grew wiser. Hand in hand, they began to mend the damage done, seeking to restore harmony with the Earth. The gods, watching from Olympus, felt pride as they saw the Earth healing and life thriving, thanks to the love humans provided.

This tale of gods and men, of love for Earth, served as a timeless reminder. To care and nurture the environment is essential, for we are part of nature's grand structure. And so, humanity continued to cherish the Earth, ensuring its beauty and bounty for generations to come.

Environment Forever Love Poem

In the heart of the cosmos, where the gods reside,
They looked upon Earth, with concern in their eyes wide.
"Look at the humans, they've lost their way,
They've forgotten that with nature, they must sway."

Down to Earth, the gods descended,
Their forms as humans, perfectly blended.

With wisdom and lessons, they began to teach,
That the love for nature was within reach.

Zeus thundered, "Respect the Earth, your home,
For from its bounty, you have grown."
Athena spoke, "Use resources with care,
Remember, it's a duty we all share."

Poseidon roared, "Keep the waters clean,
For life it nurtures, in ways unseen."
Demeter whispered, "Let the soil be,
For it gives life, to tree and bee."

Ares challenged those who wouldn't heed,
"Change your ways, or face defeat."
And so, they learned, the humans of Earth,
Of nature's value, and their own worth.

Hermes, the cunning, gave a test,
To see if humans had done their best.
A machine of destruction, he offered them,
But they chose nature, like a precious gem.

Through trials and time, the humans grew,
In their hearts, love for Earth they knew.
Hand in hand, they began to mend,
The damage done, they sought to end.

Back to Olympus, the gods returned,
Their hearts with pride, for humans, burned.
The Earth was healing, life was thriving,
Thanks to the love humans were providing.

So, here's the tale, of gods and men,
Of love for Earth, time and again.
A reminder to all, to care and nurture,
For we are part of this nature's structure.

Story 17: I Love My Morning Every Day

In the soft glow of the morning light, Emily woke from her dreams, her eyes shining bright. With hope in her heart, she greeted each day, ready to give, to love, and never sway. The morning routine was a cherished ritual, filled with smiles and sweet kisses. The energy surged within her as resilience took flight. Decisive and sure, she faced the day with might.

Birdsong echoed in the air as the breeze whispered low, creating nature's symphony. The green grass and tall trees stood as a testament to life's call. Skies of blue and seas reflecting the same, nature's beauty was ever-changing, no two days the same. Emily's heart filled with love as she began her day, cherishing everything and everyone around her.

Interconnected with nature, Emily found peace and a reflection of herself. Guided by intuition, she blended harmoniously with nature's song. Despite the hustle and bustle of modern life, nature's call cut through the noise, acting as a beacon of hope and a path to follow.

As the day ended under the starry sky, Emily appreciated the love that surrounded her. From morning to night, she roamed in nature, finding her place in the grand tapestry of life. In the quiet corners of her heart, where love and care began, she held close those she adored. Their laughter was a melody, their happiness her joy.

Small gestures like morning kisses and tender touches meant so much. Shared glances and secret smiles made every moment worthwhile. Their dreams became her guiding star, and through trials and triumphs, their love lit the way. She yearned to hold their hands in every sunrise and night's fold.

So, here's to love, pure and profound, in every heartbeat and every sound. To those Emily cherished and held dear, may her love for them always be clear, brightening each morning and every day.

I Love My Morning Everyday Poem

In the soft glow of the morning light,
We wake from dreams, eyes shining bright.
With hope in hearts, we greet the day,

Ready to give, to love, not sway.

Smiles on faces, kisses so sweet,
Love's morning ritual, a feat so neat.
Energy surges, resilience takes flight,
Decisive and sure, we ignite our might.

Birdsong's echo, the breeze whispers low,
Nature's symphony begins to flow.
The green of the grass, the trees standing tall,
A testament to life's enthralling call.

Skies of blue, seas reflecting the same,
Nature's beauty, no two days the same.
We start our day, hearts filled with love,
For all we cherish, and the heavens above.

Interconnected, in nature we find,
A reflection of self, a peace of mind.
Intuition guides, in harmony we blend,
In nature's song, our voices tend.

Modern life may cloud our sight,
Yet, nature's call cuts through the night.
A beacon of hope, a path to tread,
To our intuitive connection, we are led.

As the day ends, under the starry sheath,
We appreciate the love beneath.

Morning to night, in nature we roam,
In the grand tapestry of life, we find our home.

In the quiet corners of our hearts,
Where love resides, where care starts.
We hold them close, those we adore,
Their laughter, a melody we can't ignore.

Morning kisses, a tender touch,
Small gestures that mean so much.
A shared glance, a secret smile,
Moments that make every mile worthwhile.

In their happiness, we find our joy,
In their sorrows, our spirits buoy.
Their dreams become our guiding star,
No matter how near or far.

Through trials and triumphs, come what may,
Our love for them lights the way.
In every sunrise, in every night's fold,
It's their hands we yearn to hold.

So, here's to love, pure and profound,
In every heartbeat, in every sound.
To those we cherish, to those we hold dear,
May our love for them always be clear.

Story 18: My Oasis Love

. In the heart of the arid desert, where the sun reigns supreme and the sands stretch beyond the horizon, lies a miracle of nature, a tranquil oasis. This sanctuary of life amidst desolation was a verdant paradise defying the barrenness surrounding it.

A gentle breeze stirred the air, whispering through the palm fronds, creating a symphony of rustling leaves in the desert's profound silence. Emerald palms rose gracefully, their crowns kissing the azure sky, a stark contrast to the golden sands—a painting of nature's finest dye.

Beneath the shade, the air was cool, providing respite from the scorching heat. Here, time slowed its relentless march, and weary travelers found retreat. The heart of the oasis beat where the waters of a crystal-clear lake resided, reflecting the world outside like a liquid gem.

Fish darted in playful shoals, rippling the surface with their dance, while birdsong filled the air above in a melodious, vibrant trance. Fruits hung heavy on the boughs, offering sustenance and sweet delight—a testament to nature's bounty amidst the desert's plight.

At night, the oasis transformed under a starlit dome, becoming a vast and bright celestial theater—a secluded, peaceful home.

But lo, amidst this tranquil scene, a figure robbed in red appeared—Santaz, the desert's generous sprite, dispelling travelers' fears. With a hearty laugh and a twinkle in his eye, he bestowed gifts of joy and cheer to all who found this paradise, his presence ever near. Riding not a sleigh but a camel's back, he traversed the wide dunes, delivering dreams and hope alike beneath the desert's star.

The oasis, a haven of life, where beauty and serenity thrived, was where the soul came alive. It was a place where weary hearts found solace and dreams were nurtured in the heart of the arid desert.

My Oasis Love Poem

A gentle breeze stirs the air,
Whispering through the palm fronds,
A symphony of rustling leaves,
In the desert's profound silence.

Emerald palms rise with grace,
Their crowns kissing the azure sky,
A stark contrast to the golden sands,
A painting of nature's finest dye.

Beneath the shade, the air is cool,
A respite from the scorching heat,
Here, time slows its relentless march,
And weary travelers find retreat.

The heart of the oasis beats,
Where waters of a lake reside,
Crystal clear, a liquid gem,
Reflecting the world outside.

Fish dart in playful shoals,
Rippling the surface with their dance,
While birdsong fills the air above,
In a melodious, vibrant trance.

Fruits hang heavy on the boughs,
Offering sustenance and sweet delight,
A testament to nature's bounty,
In the midst of the desert's plight.

At night, the oasis transforms,
Under the canopy of a starlit dome,
A celestial theater, vast and bright,
In this secluded, peaceful home.

Santaz's Gift

But lo, amidst the tranquil scene,
A figure robed in red appears,
"Santaz," the desert's generous sprite,
Dispelling travelers' fears.

With a hearty laugh and a twinkle in his eye,
He bestows gifts of joy and cheer,
To all who find this paradise,
His presence ever near.

He rides not a sleigh, but a camel's back,
Across the dunes so wide and far,
Delivering dreams and hope alike,
Beneath the desert's star.

The oasis, a haven of life,
Where beauty and serenity thrive,
Amidst the endless sands of time,
It's where the soul comes alive.

Story 19: Looking for Happiness

In a forgotten land where the horizon kisses the sky, a desert was painted in amber and gold. This was the domain of Aria, a being born of sand and wind. Aria's existence was a poem, each day a verse in the endless epic of the desert. She was the whisper of the dunes, the echo of ancient caravans. Her voice, a melody, resonated with secrets of a bygone era.

One day, a traveler named Orion entered Aria's realm. A wanderer with a heavy heart, Orion sought solace in the vast desert. When he heard Aria's voice, it was as if the heavens had opened. Her words, clear and pure, were a balm to his aching spirit. Together, they embarked on a journey across the desert. Aria, the embodiment of the land, and Orion, the seeker of truth, shared stories, and dreams. The desert revealed its wonders to them: the dance of mirages, the play of light and shadow, and the night sky, a tapestry of stars.

In the heart of the desert, they found an oasis, a haven where life thrived against the arid backdrop. It was here that Orion found his purpose and Aria her companion. The desert had brought them together, two souls intertwined by destiny.

Their story became a legend, a testament to the desert's song. It was a tale of a journey that began with a poem, a child of the sun and sand who traced the whispers of the wind, and a wanderer who found his way by listening to the voice that spoke the truth beyond compare.

Looking For Happiness: An Epic Tale

In Elysium's shadow, where fables are spun,

A boy with a vision, his journey begun.
In a hamlet of silence, 'neath skies ever grey,
He dreamt of the morrow, in lands far away.

With hands stained by toil, and eyes full of gleam,
He sought the arcane, where scholars esteem.
Through tempests and whirlpools, his odyssey led,
To the citadel of sages, where his spirit was fed.

In the grandest of halls, where the wise ones convene,
He learned from the masters, in realms unseen.
His mind became a vessel for truths untold,
In the University of Stars, where legends unfold.

With a parchment of honor, his name was inscribed,
By the Archmage himself, with pride undenied.
Into the world of commerce, his path did veer,
A CEO of renown, far and near.

From the ashes of dreams, his empire rose,
A tapestry of ventures, in celestial prose.
His touch turned to gold, his vision was clear,
A fleet of stars, in the cosmic sphere.

His heart, a fountain of endless grace,
Poured out its wealth, to the human race.
Foundations of hope, he firmly laid,
For the destitute souls, in darkness wade.

To the halls of learning, he sent the young,
Where the song of knowledge is forever sung.
Yet, in his palace of solitude, high above,
He yearned for the warmth of true love.

In his quest for joy, a new chapter unfurled,
A journey through myths, in the mystical world.
A minstrel of moonlight, her voice so divine,
Brought tales of enchantment, over goblets of wine.

Together they ventured, through forests of lore,
Where unicorns roam, and griffins soar.
In the Garden of Bliss, where time stands still,
They found love's elixir, and drank their fill.

In the embrace of passion, their hearts did sing,
For happiness found, in love's eternal spring.
Through adventures grand, and moments small,
They discovered that love, is the greatest of all.

So let this tale, of a boy's quest be told,
Of seeking happiness, more precious than gold.
For in the end, it's love's sweet decree,
That unlocks the joy; and sets our hearts free.

Story 20: The Legacy of a Fisherman

In a quaint coastal village, three generations of fishermen—old Eduardo, his son Carlos, and young Mateo—lived lives intertwined with the ocean. Their days were spent on a small wooden boat, where Mateo, with the ocean in his eyes, learned the art of fishing. One fateful day, a storm struck while Mateo stayed ashore, bedridden with a fever. The village watched in despair as Eduardo and Carlos faced the tempest, but the brave boat could not withstand the fury of the waves. When calm returned, Eduardo and Carlos did not.

Left as the sole bearer of his family's legacy, Mateo grew up carrying the weight of loss and the strength of hope. He dreamt of a future where his own child's laughter would fill the void left by the sea's cruel whim. Years passed, and Mateo found solace in love. He married a woman as fierce as the ocean, and together they welcomed a son, Luca.

Honoring Eduardo and Carlos's memory, Mateo introduced Luca to fishing, restoring the old wooden boat as a testament to resilience.

Each journey was filled with stories of courage, and Luca's eyes sparkled with the same passion that had fueled generations before him. As they cast their nets beneath the vast expanse, Mateo knew the fishermen's legacy would live on—not just in their catches but in the unbreakable bond between a father, his son, and the endless sea.

FISHERMAN'S LEGACY

Upon the isle's embrace, 'neath the sky so wide,
A Fisher's tale begins, with the ocean as his guide.
His lineage cast nets, through tempest and calm tide,

In a small wooden boat, where dreams and waves
collide.

A boy amidst the sea, with his kin so dear,
Learning the water's song, that only Fishers hear.
Some days the nets would brim, some days they'd
appear,
With naught but hope's faint glimmer, and the salty air
to clear.

Years danced by, like waves upon the sand,
The boy now stood, where once he'd clung to hand.
One dawn, he stayed ashore, not joining the band,
Unknowing fate's cruel turn, that'd leave him alone on
land.

That day, the sea claimed those he held most dear,
His father and grandfather, in the depths disappeared.
The boy, now a man, shed an ocean of tear,
For the love he had lost, in the waters unclear.

In his heart, a world of fiction grew,
Where mermaids sang, and love's sweet breeze blew.
Surrounded by beauty, in hues of every hue,
A life of dreams, amidst the sea's vast blue.

So here he dwells, in the mermaid's land,
Where sorrow's touch is softened by love's gentle hand.
The Fisher's tale lives on, as the waves command,
A life of love and loss, by the ocean's strand.

The Fisher's son, once lost in mermaid's song,
Felt the call of the waves, where his heart belonged.
With a vessel modern, sleek, and strong,

He sailed the ocean, where his forefathers thronged.

The sea, once a thief, now gave him grace,
In the form of love, with a gentle face.
He found a partner, in the ocean's wide embrace,
Together, they charted life's intricate lace.

A wedding by the shore, with the horizon wide,
Promises exchanged with the ebbing tide.
The Fisher's son, with his bride by his side,
Embarked on life's journey, with the sea as their guide.

In time, a new life, from their love did spring,
A son with eyes like the ocean, in the early morning.
The Fisher's legacy, in this youngling,
Destined to learn the sea's quiet murmuring.

Together, they'd venture, as the dawn unfurls,
Father and son, casting nets in gentle swirls.
The cycle continues, as the sea swirls,
In the dance of the Fishers, with the ocean's pearls.

So the Fisher's tale grows, with each passing day,
A story of loss, love, and the sea's spray.
From the depths of sorrow, to the joyous fray,
The Fisher's line endures, come what may.

Story 21: In the Cosmic Embrace

Amidst the celestial tapestry, a lone traveler embarked on a daring odyssey, his vessel a fragile cocoon, dreams unexplored. He danced with quasars and nebulae in a cosmic waltz. Yet danger lurked—a tempest of cosmic fire, solar winds howling, black holes beckoning, and gravity's grip tightening. Fueled by stardust and wonder, he pressed on, seeking answers in the cosmic thunder.

He glimpsed her at the edge of oblivion—a vision of otherworldly grace, a celestial blur. Her eyes held galaxies, her touch electric. She cradled him, kissed his brow, and he forgot fear and pain in her embrace. Together, they danced on Mars' crimson sands, their laughter echoing across barren lands.

He marveled at her iridescent wings and her laughter's chime, feeling as if the universe conspired to intertwine their fates. He found solace and a cosmic revelation in her eyes, a love transcending time and space. He had faced death, yet in the arms of this Martian muse, he thrived anew, experiencing love's cosmic debut.

Their story was a rhapsody of an otherworldly life, a testament to the power of love in the vast expanse of the universe. They danced, laughed, and shared a bond that transcended the boundaries of the cosmos, their love story written in the stars.

The Return to Earth

Amidst the stars in cosmic lace,
A traveler ventured into space,
His vessel fragile, dreams untold,
In nebulae and quasars bold.

Danger lurked in cosmic fire,
Solar winds and black holes dire,
Gravity's grip, hope tight as thread,
Seeking answers where stardust led.

At oblivion's edge, he saw her face,
A vision of grace in a celestial place,
Her eyes held galaxies, touch electric,
A Martian muse, pure and magnetic.

She cradled him, kissed his brow,
In her arms, he forgot fear now,
On Mars' sands, they danced in light,
Their laughter echoed in the night.

Iridescent wings, laughter's chime,
As if the universe kept time,
In her eyes, he found his peace,
A cosmic love that wouldn't cease.

He faced death, yet thrived anew,
In love's debut, their bond grew,
A rhapsody of life unknown,
In star-lit paths, their love was shown.

Their story in the stars so bright,
A testament to love's pure light,
In vast expanse, they laughed, embraced,
Their love's tale, in cosmos traced.

Story 22: In the Cosmic Embrace: A Love Across Worlds

In a universe teeming with untold wonders, a lone explorer embarked on a voyage that defied the boundaries of known space. His vessel, a marvel of human engineering, carried him through the vast emptiness, past stars that shimmered like beacons in the night. He danced with the radiance of quasars, twirled with the ethereal beauty of nebulae, his journey a testament to humanity's enduring spirit of adventure.

In a universe teeming with untold wonders, a lone explorer embarked on a voyage that defied the boundaries of known space. His vessel, a marvel of human engineering, carried him through the vast emptiness, past stars that shimmered like beacons in the night. He danced with the radiance of quasars, twirled with the ethereal beauty of nebulae, his journey a testament to humanity's enduring spirit of adventure.

In a universe teeming with untold wonders, a lone explorer embarked on a voyage that defied the boundaries of known space. His vessel, a marvel of human engineering, carried him through the vast emptiness, past stars that shimmered like beacons in the night. He danced with the radiance of quasars, twirled with the ethereal beauty of nebulae, his journey a testament to humanity's enduring spirit of adventure.

Yet, amidst the beauty, danger awaited. A storm of cosmic fire raged, solar winds howled their deadly warnings, black holes whispered their promises of oblivion, and gravity's relentless pull threatened to end his quest. But he was undeterred, his heart fueled by the magic of stardust and an insatiable curiosity.

Yet, amidst the beauty, danger awaited. A storm of cosmic fire raged, solar winds howled their deadly warnings, black holes whispered their promises of oblivion, and gravity's relentless pull threatened to end his quest. But he was undeterred, his heart fueled by the magic of stardust and an insatiable curiosity.

Yet, amidst the beauty, danger awaited. A storm of cosmic fire raged, solar winds howled their deadly warnings, black holes whispered their promises of oblivion, and gravity's relentless pull threatened to end his quest. But he was undeterred, his heart fueled by the magic of stardust and an insatiable curiosity.

At the very brink of destruction, he saw her. An otherworldly vision, her presence was a beacon of light in the darkness. Her eyes held the secrets of galaxies, her touch was a spark of life. She cradled him, kissed his brow, and in her embrace, he found a peace he had never known. They danced on Mars' crimson sands, their laughter a symphony that echoed through the barren landscape, their love a force that transcended time and space.

At the very brink of destruction, he saw her. An otherworldly vision, her presence was a beacon of light in the darkness. Her eyes held the secrets of galaxies, her touch was a spark of life. She cradled him, kissed his brow, and in her embrace, he found a peace he had never known. They danced on Mars' crimson sands, their laughter a symphony that echoed through the barren landscape, their love a force that transcended time and space.

At the very brink of destruction, he saw her. An otherworldly vision, her presence was a beacon of light in the darkness. Her eyes held the secrets of galaxies, her touch was a spark of life. She cradled him, kissed his brow, and in her embrace, he found a peace he had never known. They danced on Mars' crimson sands, their laughter a symphony that echoed through the barren landscape, their love a force that transcended time and space.

Together, they etched their story into the very fabric of the cosmos, a tale of love and bravery that would shine bright for all eternity. Their journey was not just a dance through the stars, but a testament to the boundless possibilities of the human spirit and the enduring power of love.

Together, they etched their story into the very fabric of the cosmos, a tale of love and bravery that would shine bright for all eternity. Their journey was not just a dance through the stars, but a testament to the boundless possibilities of the human spirit and the enduring power of love.

Together, they etched their story into the very fabric of the cosmos, a tale of love and bravery that would shine bright for all eternity. Their journey was not just a dance through the stars, but a testament to the boundless possibilities of the human spirit and the enduring power of love.

Amidst the vast celestial sea,
A traveler embarked on a daring spree,
His vessel a cocoon, dreams yet untold,
He soared through stars, a story bold.

With quasars he danced, nebulae he twirled,
A cosmic ballet in the void, unfurled.
Yet danger lurked, a tempest dire,
Cosmic fire, a threatening pyre.

Solar winds howled, black holes called,
Gravity's grip, hope nearly stalled.
But fueled by stardust and endless wonder,
He sought the truth in cosmic thunder.

At oblivion's edge, her vision appeared,
A Martian muse, her grace revered.
Eyes held galaxies, touch electric,
A celestial bond, pure and magnetic.

She cradled him, kissed his brow,
Cosmic dust on lips, a promise now.
In her embrace, fear and pain ceased, An otherworldly
life, his heart released.

Together they danced on Mars' crimson sand,
Laughter echoing in the barren land.
He marveled at wings and laughter's chime,
Their fates entwined in cosmic rhyme.

In her eyes, solace and revelation,
Love transcending time and gravitation.
In her arms, he thrived anew,
Love's cosmic debut, pure and true.

Their story etched in stardust bright,
A symphony of constellations, a celestial light.
In the cosmos vast, they'd forever dwell,
Two souls entwined—a celestial tale to tell.

Story 23: A Journey from Geneva to Malaga

Above the Alps, my flight begins. Swissair wings through the sky, spinning. From Geneva's snowy land to Malaga's sunlit coast, the cabin's hum sings a soothing song as we glide among the clouds. The mountains shrink beneath me, heading south to where warm winds await. This journey, with hopes so high, carried by Swiss precision, crosses from the land of time's own keep to Andalusia's deep shores.

On May 19th, a clear day, my heart takes flight, leaving all fear. Swissair surely carries me to Spanish lands, alluring and pure. From Geneva's calm to Malaga's charm, this journey is part of my travel balm, bridging across the blue, bringing dreams and new adventures.

To my palace home, I return alone—no wife, no kin, just silent stone. But there to greet me, a love not small—my faithful pet, Hunter, above all. He fills the halls with pure delight with a wagging tail and bright eyes. Though my family is far in the USA, Hunter's love lights up my day.

In this grand abode, where echoes roam, I find the warmth of a true home. For Hunter's care, so full and free, brings back the joy meant to be. Together, we create a haven of love and happiness, proving that home is not just a place, but the company we keep.

Above the Alps, my flight begins,
Swissair wings, through the sky, it spins.
From Geneva's land of snowy white,
To Malaga's coast, where the sun shines bright.

The cabin's hum, a soothing song,
As we glide the clouds along.
Mountains shrink beneath me far,
Heading south, to where the warm winds are.

A journey's start, with hopes so high,
Swiss precision, through the sky.
From the land of time's own keep,
To Andalusia's shores, so deep.

May 19th, the day so clear,
My heart takes flight, leaving all fear.
Swissair takes me, on wings so sure,
To Spanish lands, with allure pure.

From Geneva's calm, to Malaga's charm,
The journey's part of the travel's balm.
Swissair, my bridge, across the blue,
Bringing dreams and adventures new.

To my palace home, I return alone,
No wife, no kin, just silent stone.
But there, to greet me, love not small,
My faithful pet, Hunter, above all.

With wagging tail and eyes so bright,
He fills the halls with pure delight.

Though family's far, in the USA,
Hunter's love lights up my day.

In this grand abode, where echoes roam,
I find the warmth of a true home.
For Hunter's care, so full and free,
Brings back the joy that's meant to be.

So here I stand, in my palace grand,
With Hunter's head beneath my hand.
In this moment, no more to roam,
I'm truly glad to be back home.

Story 24: Forests Fighting for Survival

In the heart of a vast forest, the trees wept, lifting their branches to the sky in a silent plea for mercy. They whispered to the breeze, begging for salvation from the humans who cut and burned without care. Torrential rains fell, but it was not water that poured down—it was flames that roared, consuming the once lush and wide green canopy. Human pride had turned the forest into a victim.

The trees cried out to the divine, asking for humans to be instilled with a sense of love. The trees' survival was intertwined with that of humans, a shared dance of life.

By reducing the forest, humans sealed their own fate. The trees' message was clear: They hoped human minds would relent.

The trees were the Earth's lungs, essential for life to stand. The plea was to protect them and let life's bell chime. Amid this tale of woe, there shone a beacon of hope. A noble few humans stood steadfast and true, fighting for the trees. They formed a strong alliance to guard the forests against demise. Each year, their ranks grew, igniting change and compelling lawmakers to act.

New laws were born, creating a creed of protection for every tree. Thanks to these guardians of the leaf, the forests began to breathe a sigh of relief. The story spread, inspiring many to join the valiant fight. Together, they stood hand in hand, determined to save the forests and heal the land.

Through unity and determination, the alliance proved that humanity could protect the Earth's green lungs and ensure a bright future for all.

Forests Fighting for Survival

In the forest's heart, the trees weep,
Lifting branches to the skies so deep.
A plea for mercy, they silently cry,
To the divine above, they raise their sigh.

"Save us," they whisper to the breeze,
From the humans who do as they please.

Cutting and burning, they show no care,
For the brothers and sisters we cannot spare.

The rains come down, a torrential pour,
Yet it's not water, but flames that roar.
Our green canopy, once lush and wide,
Now falls victim to human pride.

Hear our call, O mighty God above,
Instill in humans the sense to love.
For our survival intertwines with theirs,
In this dance of life, a shared affairs.

By reducing us, they seal their fate,
An act so blind, a needless hate.
Our cry is clear, our message sent,
In hopes their minds will finally relent.

For we are the lungs of this Earth so grand,
Without us, life cannot stand.
So hear our plea, O children of time,
Protect us all, and let life's bell chime

Yet in this tale of woe and plight,
There shines a beacon of hopeful light.
Some humans stand, a noble few,
Who fight for the trees, steadfast and true.

They've formed an alliance, strong and wise,
To guard the forests 'against demise.
With every year, their ranks swell,
A global force, their hearts compel.

In lands afar, they've made their mark,

Igniting change, a vital spark.
Their influence grows, a rising tide,
As lawmakers heed the call outside.

New laws are born, protection's creed,
For every tree, in word and deed.
The forests breathe, a sigh of relief,
Thanks to the guardians of the leaf.

So let us join this valiant fight,
For trees, for life, for future bright.
Together we'll stand, hand in hand,
To save the forests; and heal the land.

Story 25: Whispers of Marbella

In Marbella's El Conche mountain, where sun and sea conspire, lies a hidden grove sanctuary untouched by time. A cottage, with timeworn stones bathed in golden hues and a terracotta roof, shelters secrets whispered by the wind. Here, I retreat, seeking solace and forgotten tales. Bouchelo, the old hound, greets me, his eyes like ancient constellations. Mello, the mischievous fox, dances ahead, his russet fur a streak of wildfire. The enigmatic cat, Natacha, slinks along gnarled olive roots, her eyes reflecting moonlight and mystery.

Together, we unravel existence—past laughter and tears, future strokes of destiny. In the grove's heart, a gnarled pine stands sentinel, cradling secrets of generations. The pine remembers forgotten vows, lost dreams, and unspoken confessions, its silvered needles rustling in the breeze.

Sitting against the ancient trunk, I listen to the sea's lullaby—a melody of longing and belonging. The waves kiss the shore, leaving behind fragments of forgotten stories. The grove comes alive with whispers of lovers who once sought refuge, their names etched into bark. Moonlit rituals, nymphs and faeries, stolen kisses and promises made beneath star-studded canopies—these tales defy reason.

I wonder if those lovers, reborn in different skins, are drawn back to this sacred ground. Perhaps they walk among us—the fig-seller, the fisherman, the artist. Their eyes, haunted by memories, seek recognition.

As the sun dips low, casting shadows on the cottage walls, I vow to honor the past, embrace the present, and step into unwritten chapters. Bouchelo rests his head on my lap, Mello curls at my feet, and Natcha weaves circles around us. We become part of the grove—a living ode to time's passage. In the fading light, I raise my gaze to the whispering pines, their ancient voices blending with my chorus of hope, resilience, and the quest for meaning.

Whispers of Marbella

Upon Marbella's El Conche mountain's crest,
I rest, Where sun and sea converge, their secrets
unexpressed.
My cottage, weathered stones kissed by golden light,
Holds memories—theirs and mine—woven through the
night.

Bouchelo, loyal hound, his eyes like constellations
bright,   Maps the dew-kissed grass,
tracing paths of ancient might.
Mello, russet fox, dances wild, a flame against the
green,
While Natcha, a feline muse, weaves moonbeams
unseen.

In this fleeting moment, past and future intertwine,
The sea's eternal song, a lullaby, a timeless sign.
Life's symphony echoes—the laughter, the tears,
And I, seeker of forgotten tales, listen as it nears.

The gnarled pine stands sentinel, its whispers true,
Keeper of vows, lost dreams, and love's residue.
Did lovers once pledge beneath its ancient boughs?
Their souls, reborn, perhaps walk among us now.

As sun dips low, shadows stretch across the land,
I vow to honor the past, embrace the present's hand.

Bouchelo rests, Mello curls, Natcha weaves her spell,
And the whispering pines echo stories we can't tell.

So here, in Marbella's embrace, I find my rhyme,
Where El Conche's mountain meets the sea's sublime.
Life's rhythm pulses—past, present, future's call,
And I, a wanderer, surrender to its sweet enthrall.

Story 26: The Importance of Women in Men's Existence

In a quaint village, as the sun painted the sky at dawn, lived a woman named Khadeja. Her presence was like a gentle breeze, carrying the scent of blooming jasmine through narrow cobblestone streets. Khadeja's laughter resonated within her family home from her earliest days, a melody of joy and innocence.

As Khadeja grew, her grace and wisdom blossomed like village flowers. She naturally became a teacher, guiding her younger siblings with patience and love. Her lessons were woven into everyday life—kindness through actions, strength through resolve, and love through unwavering support.

As a wife, Khadeja brought light into her husband's world. Her love guided him through life's storms, making their home a sanctuary of happiness and warmth. As a mother, she molded her children with compassion and discipline, being their first teacher, constant cheerleader, and soft pillow for weary heads. Her sacrifices were silent, but her love was as palpable as the morning sun.

Khadeja's husband found strength in her roots; she was his nourishing soil, quenching rain, and life-giving sun. In her embrace, he found peace, seeing his best self-reflected in her gaze.

The village often whispered about the secret to Khadeja's family's happiness. They saw her children grow into leaders, her husband prosper, and their home flourish. The answer was clear: Khadeja was the cornerstone of their existence.

Khadeja's story is a tribute to all women. They are the world's comfort, guidance, and strength. Women are the unsung heroines, shaping the present and future with their gentle power

The Importance of Women in Our Existence

In the tapestry of life, a thread runs true,
The vibrant hue of a woman's virtue.
From a girl whose laughter fills the air,
To the strength of a woman's nurturing care.

In her youth, a joyous melody plays,
Gentleness in her gaze, brightening days.
As she grows, her wisdom takes its place,
Educating, loving, with elegance and grace.

A mother's touch, a home's beating heart,
In every family, she plays a central part.
Raising children with a tender hand,
Guiding them to understand.

Love she gives, without measure or end,
Supporting her partner, an unwavering friend.
Sacrifices made, her happiness she lends,
To family, she's the anchor, on which it depends.

So, here's to the women, in all their forms,
The calm in our storms, the warmth when it warms.
For without them, our lives would be less,
They are our happiness, our core, our fortress.

STORY 27: PEACE & UNITY

As the Creator observed the turmoil below, a profound sadness enveloped the heavens. Amidst the chaos, a glimmer of hope persisted. In a small village untouched by war, individuals gathered with a shared vision of peace. They spoke of understanding and compassion, advocating for the investment in prosperity rather than destruction. Their words, like seeds, took root in the hearts of those yearning for change.

Over the years, these ideas blossomed into movements. People from different nations, speaking varied tongues, began to lay down their arms. They met on fields once used for battle, not to fight but to build. Schools, hospitals, and gardens replaced remnants of conflict.

The paradigm shifted from conquest to collaboration. Wealth was now measured by community well-being and the laughter of children.

The Creator, watching from above, saw humanity's potential realized. The brain, given to think and to be fair, was finally being used for its true purpose. War and peace took a new turn, with peace becoming a tangible reality. This new world was crafted by the hands and hearts of those who dared to envision a better future.

The story of transformation spread far and wide, inspiring others to join the cause. The collective efforts of these individuals created a legacy of hope and resilience, proving that peace was not just a fleeting dream but a reality achievable through compassion and collaboration. The Creator's sadness was replaced by a profound sense of pride, witnessing the dawn of a new era of harmony and understanding

Peace and Unity

In a world torn by war's relentless rage,
A village stood, untouched by time's cruel page.
Here, hearts united, dreaming of peace,
Where love prevails and all conflicts cease.

From history's dawn, resources drained,
Not for life's gain, but by greed stained.

Yet, in this haven, a new game's played,
Where swords to plowshares are swiftly swayed.

Words of harmony, like seeds sown wide,
Across the lands, they spread far and wide.
Fields of battle, now grounds to heal,
With schools and laughter, a better deal.

The game of old, of wealth and land,
Gave way to a new, a united stand.
Children's mirth, the truest wealth,
In every smile, life's sweetest health.

The Creator's query from skies so vast,
"Did I make man for this bloodshed cast?"
Now sees an answer, in deeds so fair,
Humanity's potential finally laid bare.

So let this poem of peace resound,
In every heart, let love be found.
For in each verse, a hope's embraced,
In every rhyme, war's shadows eased.

Story 28: THE ARAB SPRING OF 2011

Here's a short story inspired by the spirit of the Arab Spring:
A spark of defiance ignited in the heart of the old city, where the scent of jasmine lingered in the air and the

call to prayer echoed off ancient walls. It began in Tunisia, a flame fanned by the winds of change,

spreading to Libya, Egypt, Syria, and Yemen. These were lands of contrast, where peace and turmoil walked hand in hand. The people, who once found solace in daily bread and the comfort of community, now yearned for a voice in the destiny of their nations. They were governed by rulers who seemed more deity than human, their wills inscribed upon the sands of time. But the Arab Spring came, a tempest of hope and upheaval. It toppled the old guards, their statues crashing down like the walls of Jericho. From the rubble rose not one, not two, but hundreds of voices, each clamoring to be heard, to shape the future

The aftermath was a mosaic of triumph and tragedy. The old order was shattered, leaving a vacuum where once there was certainty. Gangs and thieves vied for power in the absence of law, and the streets became a battleground for competing ideals. Amidst the chaos, millions fled, seeking refuge across treacherous seas and distant borders.

They carried with them stories of a home lost to strife, their hearts heavy with the weight of memory. Yet, even as the countries grappled with their newfound freedom, the spirit of the Arab Spring endured. It lived in the courage of those who stood for justice, in the resilience of communities rebuilding from the ashes, and in the unwavering belief that a garden of peace could one day bloom from the seeds of revolution.

The ARAB SPRING of 2011

From Tunis' heart, a spark was lit,
A flame of change, that wouldn't quit.
It danced through Libya's ancient sands,
And touched the hearts in Egypt's lands.

In Syria's streets, it roared with might,
In Yemen's nights, a beacon bright.
A spring of souls, yearning to be free,
From the grip of gods, they sought the key.

The rulers fell, their thrones undone,
As people rose with the rising sun.
But in the void, chaos found its place,
And peace was lost, in a frantic chase.

Gangs and thieves, in power's game,
Left countries torn, and never the same.
The sea swallowed dreams, in waves so cruel,
As millions fled, from a homegrown duel.

Yet, amidst the dark, a hope still gleams,
For unity's light, and peace's dreams.
The Arab Spring, with all its pain,
Reminds us all, of freedom's gain.

Story 29: Beyond the Horizon-1

Beyond the horizon, he roamed the seas, crossing continents, chasing dreams in the breeze. Desolate deserts, rugged peaks so high, A quest for love beneath the endless sky.

Weeks turned to months, his heart aflame, seeking love's sweet whisper, a timeless name. Each sunrise whispered secrets untold, guided by the compass of love's gold.

Amid twilight's tender grace, he found her face, A star in the vast, endless embrace. Her eyes, galaxies of wonder and light, their souls entwined, dancing through the night.

He sang of joy, love's sweet refrain, their laughter echoed across the plain. Yet, as the moon wept silver tears, He pondered what lay beyond love's frontiers.

Happiness, a fleeting comet's flight, dancing on the edge of day and night. In her touch, her whispered name, Or quiet moments, hearts aflame.

Perhaps happiness was the journey itself, the winding path, the longing felt. Vowed to cherish each stolen kiss, Savoring love's nectar, eternal bliss.

Wove their tale in stardust threads, two souls bound by celestial spreads. Beyond continents, seas, and endless skies, we found eternity in each other's eyes.

Traced her skin, a cartographer's delight, Lost in passion's labyrinth, burning bright. Yet shadows crept, doubts whispered near, Was happiness a fleeting comet here?

Sought answers were in her eyes' reflection, and the Universe was mirrored in their connection. Tender ache when love blooms fierce, Hearts wide awake, passion's pierce.

Wandered, hand in hand, through painted sand, Each grain a memory, love's climb so grand. Happiness, not a place to find, But the journey, love intertwined.

Beyond the horizon, he roamed the seas,
Crossing continents, chasing dreams in the breeze.
Desolate deserts, rugged peaks so high,
A quest for love beneath the endless sky.

Weeks turned to months, his heart aflame,
Seeking love's sweet whisper, a timeless name.
Each sunrise whispered secrets untold,
Guided by the compass of love's gold.

Amid twilight's tender grace, he found her face,
A star in the vast, endless embrace.
Her eyes, galaxies of wonder and light,
Their souls entwined, dancing through the night.

He sang of joy, love's sweet refrain,
Their laughter echoed across the plain.
Yet, as the moon wept silver tears,
He pondered what lay beyond love's frontiers.

Happiness, a fleeting comet's flight,
Dancing on the edge of day and night.
In her touch, her whispered name,
Or quiet moments, hearts aflame.

Perhaps happiness was the journey itself,
The winding path, the longing felt.
Vowed to cherish each stolen kiss,
Savoring love's nectar, eternal bliss.

Wove their tale in stardust threads,
Two souls bound by celestial spreads.
Beyond continents, seas, endless skies,
Found eternity in each other's eyes.

Traced her skin, a cartographer's delight,
Lost in passion's labyrinth, burning bright.
Yet shadows crept, doubts whispered near,
Was happiness a fleeting comet here?

Sought answers in her eyes' reflection,
Universe mirrored in their connection.
Tender ache when love blooms fierce,
Hearts wide awake, passion's pierce.

Wandered, hand in hand, through painted sand,
Each grain a memory, love's climb so grand.
Happiness, not a place to find,
But the journey, love intertwined.

Story 30: A Symphony of Love

In the quiet hours of dawn, she stirs—a conductor of love, her heart's sweet refrain. Her hands, like gentle bows on strings, weave melodies of care. Her smile is the first note in our family's song as she rises with the sun. The kitchen hums, and love brews in the warmth where we belong. Through breakfast chaos, she pirouettes between tasks with grace, her laughter echoing like a lilting piano melody.

In the afternoon hush, she tends to bloom, nurturing life with a gardener's whispered secret. When twilight paints the sky, she gathers us close, her voice a soothing cello's resonance, guiding us to dreams. Around the dinner table, we gather—a symphony of forks and laughter. Her recipes compose a feast that warms our hearts each night.

As moonlight spills across our bed, she whispers love notes. Her touch, a violin's tender vibrato, plays the music of forever. In whispered moments, our hearts unite in gratitude. The children's laughter, like wind chimes, carries her name, reflecting her grace. Her lap is a sanctuary for dreams, where love blooms perennially.

Woven into every thread, her legacy is stitched with resilience and care. She's the seamstress of our family tapestry. We raise our voices with grateful hearts, for she's the symphony that makes us whole. In the quiet chambers of her mind, love's melody forever remains, even as memories fade. Her eyes now hold constellations of lost stars, as children gather around, soothing her with stories and shared laughter.

They guide her through forgotten gardens, honoring her legacy. They weave time's threads, stitching moments anew. Around the table, they share meals, laugh, and hold her gaze. In the quiet of nightfall, they whisper reassurance, her name a prayer on their lips.

We raise our voices in a grateful chorus, for she is the heart of our family's symphony. Children care for her as she once did, their gratitude blooming in every gesture. A symphony of love in this sacred space.

Fading Notes of Remembrance

In dawn's quiet hours, she gently stirs,
A conductor of love, her heart's sweet refrain,
Her hands, like bows on strings, weave care,
Melodies in our family's domain.

Rising with the sun, her smile's the start,
Of our family's song, the first, bright note,
The kitchen hums, love brews in its heart,
In warmth, our day's symphony she wrote.

Through breakfast chaos, she pirouettes,
Tasks with grace, laughter's piano song,
Afternoon hush, tending blooms she sets,
Gardener's secret whispers all day long.

At twilight's fall, she gathers us near,
Her voice, a cello's soothing embrace,
Guides us to dreams, no worries, no fear,
Around the table, forks and laughter trace.

Moonlight spills on our shared bed,
She whispers love notes in the dark,
Her touch, a violin's tender thread,
Plays music of forever, a heartfelt spark.

Children's laughter, like wind chimes, sings,
Her name a melody, reflecting grace,
Her lap, a dream's sanctuary, brings,
Perennial love blooms in this place.

Her legacy, resilience and care,
Woven in every thread, we see,
The seamstress of our family's fare,
Her love, the symphony's key.

In quiet chambers of her mind,
Love's melody forever stays,
Even as memories blur and bind,
Her children's stories, her heart sways.

In nightfall's hush, whispers reassure,
Her name a prayer on our lips,
We raise our voices, grateful and pure,
For she's our symphony's heart, love's eclipse.

Children care as she once did,
Gratitude blooms in every space,
A symphony of love, in actions hid,
In this sacred, loving place.

Story 32: Two Lovers in Twilight

In a quaint neighborhood where cobblestone streets whispered secrets, a girl of seventeen summers discovered love. Her heart fluttered like a fragile butterfly for her neighbor, a boy with eyes like the ocean. Fate intervened, and they parted ways, each seeking knowledge in distant lands. Years flowed, carving memories, as the girl's dreams were painted with hues of longing. She wondered if he, too, carried her image across oceans and through textbooks.

As if orchestrated by destiny, they returned—wiser and weathered by time. Their eyes met, recognition sparking flames and rekindling an ancient connection. From the first glance, they knew their hearts had been entwined for years. They danced through seasons, shared laughter, tears, and whispered vows. Their love, a symphony composed by fate, culminated in a wedding beneath blossoming trees.

In their cozy home, they built a nest filled with laughter and morning coffee scented with promises. He, the steady oak carved by life's tempests, and she, the wildflower dancing in his shelter, weathered storms, and sunsets together. Their love was a compass guiding them home.

Early mornings found her silhouette against the window as she brewed love into steaming cups. They sat side by side, savoring the quiet before the day's rush. Hand in hand, they explored the world, her laughter echoing through narrow alleys, his eyes capturing her joy. They climbed mountains, their breaths mingling, and their love anchored them against life's uncertainties.

One day, a tiny heartbeat within her multiplied their love. Nights blurred into diaper changes and giggles, their hearts expanding with each sleepless hour. Time etched lines on their faces, yet their love remained unwavering. He surprised her with wildflowers, she traced constellations on his skin. They sat on the porch swing, reminiscing about their first encounter, laughing at fate's matchmaking.

Their love story became folklore, whispered by young lovers under moonlight. He passed away first, leaving her aching, and she followed, chasing his shadow. Their legacy lingered; a house filled with memories, children carrying their laughter, and a love that transcended time, eternally entwined in the quiet corners of that quaint neighborhood.

Two Lovers in Twilight

In the quiet corners of a quaint neighborhood,
Where cobblestone streets whispered secrets,
A girl of seventeen summers found love,
Her heart fluttered like a fragile butterfly's glove.

Her neighbor, a boy with ocean eyes,
Saw her affection, though unspoken ties,
Fate played its hand, they parted ways,
Each seeking knowledge in distant days.

Years flowed like a river, carving dreams,
The girl's heart painted with longing's gleams,
She wondered if he, too, carried her light,
Across oceans, through books, in the night.

Destiny's hand returned them in time,
Wiser, weathered, their hearts in rhyme,
Eyes met, sparks flew, flames rekindled,
Two souls, ancient connection, rekindled.

From the first glance, they knew their hearts, Entwined
for years, a love story's start, Etched in constellations,
waiting its chapter, Reunited, they danced, hearts
enraptured.

Through seasons, hand in hand they roamed,
Shared laughter, tears, whispered vows at home,
A symphony of fate, beneath blossoming trees,
Their love, a melody, carried on the breeze.

In cozy corners, they built a nest,
Laughter echoed, sun-kissed walls blessed,
Morning coffee, promises made anew,
Evenings wrapped in stories they drew.

He, the steady oak, life's tempests faced,
She, the wildflower, in his shelter embraced,
Weathered storms, sunsets, love their guide,
A compass home, where hearts reside.

Early mornings, her silhouette in light,
Brewing love, steaming cups, so bright,
Side by side, kitchen table calm,
Traced the rim of her mug, a silent psalm.

Hand in hand, explored the world's view,
Ancient ruins, bustling markets, too,
Laughter echoed through alleys narrow,
Eyes captured joy, love an arrow.

Climbed mountains, breaths intertwined,
Steadying each other, secrets combined,
Love, an anchor against life's storms,
Together, weathered, transformed.

Tiny heartbeat, love multiplied,
Miracle unfolding, eyes open wide,
Bedtime stories, whispers so sweet,
Cradled child, love's gentle beat.

Nights blurred, sleepless hours shared,
Strength marveled, grace declared,
Solace in arms, weary but content,
Love remained, time's testament.

Lines etched on faces, love unwavering,
Wildflowers, constellations, still savoring,
Porch swing, hands entwined, sunset's hue,
Reminiscing first encounter, laughter's cue.

Love story folklore, whispered by moonlight,
Legacy lingered, memories bright,

Children's laughter, love's eternal sign,
In the quiet corners, always intertwined.

Story 32: Beyond The Horizon-2

He crossed continents, seas, and skies, Chasing whispers of love's sweet guise. Through deserts desolate and peaks so high, His heart yearned for love nearby.

Days turned to weeks, months unfurled, His soul aflame, a quest in this world. Each sunrise whispered secrets untold; He followed the compass of love's bold.

Amidst twilight's tender grace, He found her in a vast embrace. Her eyes, galaxies of wonder bright, their souls entwined, danced through the night.

He sang of joy, love's sweet refrain, their laughter echoing across the plain. Yet, as the moon wept silver tears, He pondered love's frontiers.

Like a comet's flight, happiness danced on the edge of day and night. In her touch, her whispered name, in quiet moments, hearts aflame.

Perhaps happiness was the journey, the winding path, the longing felt. He vowed to cherish every kiss, to savor love's eternal bliss.

So, they wove their tale in stardust threads, two souls bound by love's spreads. They found eternity in each other's eyes beyond continents, seas, and endless skies.

He wove her laughter into constellations, mapping galaxies of shared elations. Their love, a symphony of whispered sighs, echoing across cerulean skies.

In moon-kissed nights, they danced as one, two souls entangled, destinies spun. He traced her skin, desire's cartographer, Lost in passion's fire.

Shadows crept like silent thieves, and Doubts whispered through autumn leaves. Was happiness a comet's flight, or a steady flame through night?

In her eyes' reflection, he sought the universe mirrored in their connection. Happiness, a tender ache, when love blooms fiercely, hearts awake.

Hand in hand, through sunsets, memories are set on shifting sand. Beyond continents, endless skies, their love story lies in stardust.

He realized that happiness was not a place but the embrace. The journey, the love they chose, in twilight's grace, their story rose.

Beyond The Horizon

He crossed continents, seas, and skies,
Chasing whispers of love's sweet guise.
Through deserts desolate and peaks so high,
His heart yearned for love nearby.

Days turned to weeks, months unfurled,
His soul aflame, a quest in this world.
Each sunrise whispered secrets untold,
He followed the compass of love's bold.

Amidst twilight's tender grace,
He found her in a vast embrace.
Her eyes, galaxies of wonder bright,
Their souls entwined, danced through night.

He sang of joy, love's sweet refrain,
Their laughter echoing across the plain.
Yet, as the moon wept silver tears,
He pondered love's frontiers.

Happiness, like a comet's flight,
Danced on the edge of day and night.
In her touch, her whispered name,
In quiet moments, hearts aflame.

Perhaps happiness was the journey,
The winding path, the longing felt.
He vowed to cherish every kiss,
To savor love's eternal bliss.

So, they wove their tale in stardust threads,
Two souls bound by love's spreads.
Beyond continents, seas, and endless skies,
They found eternity in each other's eyes.

He wove her laughter into constellations,
Mapping galaxies of shared elations.
Their love, a symphony of whispered sighs,
across cerulean skies.

In moon-kissed nights, they danced as one,
Two souls entangled, destinies spun.
He traced her skin, desire's cartographer,
Lost in passion's fire.

Shadows crept like silent thieves,
Doubts whispered through autumn leaves.
Was happiness a comet's flight,
Or a steady flame through night?

In her eyes' reflection, he sought,
The universe mirrored in their connection.
Happiness, a tender ache,
When love blooms fierce, hearts awake.

Hand in hand, through sunsets,
On shifting sand, memories set.
Beyond continents, endless skies,
Their love story in stardust lies.

Happiness, he realized,
Was not a place, but the embrace.
The journey, the love they chose,
In twilight's grace, their story rose.

Story 33: In The Quiet of Geneva's Embrace

n the hushed serenity of Geneva, where the mountains touched the heavens and the lakes mirrored the sky, a young couple sought refuge. Beneath the watchful gaze of stars, they found solace in the city's embrace. Once faltering like a hesitant breeze, their love now yearned for reconciliation and renewal.

One night, under the canopy of twinkling constellations, they walked hand in hand along the cobblestone streets. The air was filled with the scent of blooming flowers and the distant hum of city life. He stopped suddenly, his voice soft yet resolute, "I offer these words, a tender lace, to heal the hurt, to close the space."

She listened, her heart beating to the rhythm of his sincere apology. "My love, for the doubts I let slip, for the shadows that made our trust dip, I am deeply sorry for the falter, the trip, in this journey of our partnership."

His eyes, reflecting the steadfast Alps, held a promise. "Like the mountains stand firm and true, my feelings for you are ever anew. Through the changing seasons and morning dew, my heart remains forever due."

Tears glistened in her eyes, and she whispered, "Forgive the storm that clouded sight. You are my daybreak, my light. Together, let's reach new height, in love's endless flight, so bright."

They embraced, their hearts beating in unison. The city around them seemed to glow with newfound warmth, as if blessing their renewed bond. In that quiet moment, beneath Geneva's embrace, they discovered that love, though tested by time and trials, could rise above all.

Together, they vowed to cherish each moment, to weather any storm, and to dance through life's myriad rhythms with a love that was steadfast, unyielding, and ever true.

In The Quiet of Geneva's Embrace

In the quiet of Geneva's embrace,
Under the watchful stars' trace,
I offer words, a tender lace,
To heal the hurt, to close the space.

My love, for doubts that I let slip,
For shadows that made our trust dip,
I'm sorry for the falter, the trip,
In this journey of our partnership.

Like the Alps stand firm and true,

My feelings for you, ever anew,
Through seasons' change and morning dew,
My heart, to you, forever due.

Forgive the storm that clouded sight,
For you are my daybreak, my light,
Together, let's reach new height,
In love's endless flight, so bright.

Story 34: The Pillar of the House

Magdy lived in the vibrant town of Harmony, known for the laughter from his home and the blooming garden. Magdy was the pillar of his family, a foundation of balance and prosperity. His days began before dawn, preparing breakfast for his wife Randa, a teacher, and their children, Didi and Orion. Magdy believed in the importance of starting the day together, sharing plans over freshly baked bread.

Actions spoke louder than words for Magdy. After the morning hustle, he crafted furniture in his workshop, each piece filled with love and memories for their home. He valued community, often helping neighbors and teaching his children the importance of service. Prosperity, he taught, was not in material wealth but in relationships and joy from simple pleasures.

As the sun set, warmth filled Magdy's home, not just from the hearth but from family bonds. They shared triumphs and trials, finding strength in one another.

Magdy listened, advised, and offered comfort, reminding his family they were never alone.

Years passed, and the children grew, carrying their father's lessons. They ventured into the world, creating their own paths while maintaining the balance and prosperity of their upbringing. Magdy and Randa watched with pride, knowing they had nurtured a family that understood the true essence of wealth.

Magdy remained the silent hero, the gardener of life's most precious blooms—his family. His legacy was not just in the furniture he crafted or the garden he tended, but in the values and love he instilled in his family, making their home a sanctuary of warmth and togetherness.

In the vibrant town of Harmony,
Lived Magdy, known for family's glee.
Not for wealth or career acclaim,
But laughter from his home's warm flame.

He was the pillar, firm and true,
Balance and prosperity, he knew.
Days began before dawn's first light,
With breakfast, love, and plans so bright.

His wife, Randa, minds did mold,
dreams as big as bold.
Actions spoke where words fell short,
Crafted furniture, love's support.

Each piece a story, memory grand,
A legacy built by Magdy's hand.
Believed in community's strength and grace,
Teaching service, joy's embrace.

Not wealth in gold, but bonds so strong,
In simple pleasures, life's sweet song.
As the sun set, warmth filled their space,
Bonds of family, love's embrace.

Triumphs, trials, they'd share each night,
Finding strength in each other's light.
Magdy listened, held their hands,
A silent hero, love's commands.

Years rolled on, children grew,
Paths of their own, lessons true.
Magdy and Randa, pride did swell,
A family's essence, they did well.

Silent hero, gardener bright,
Of life's blooms, morning to night.
Prosperity in love's rich seams,
Magdy's legacy, life's pure dreams.

Disclosure:

Verlag: BoD · Books on Demand GmbH,
Überseering 33, 22297 Hamburg, bod@bod.de
Druck: Libri Plureos GmbH, Friedensallee 273,
22763 Hamburg
ISBN: 978-3-7693-4034-1